COMMITMENT TO A DECEITFUL LIAR

Jenelle Simpson

This is a work of creative nonfiction. Some parts have been fictionalized in varying degrees, for various purposes. The events and conversations in this book have been set down to the best of the author's ability, although some names and details have been changed to protect the privacy of individuals.

Copyright © 2021 by Jenelle Simpson

All rights reserved. No part of this book may be reproduced or used in any manner without written permission of the copyright owner except for the use of quotations in a book review.
For more information, address: info@jenellesimpson.com

First paperback edition December 2021
First hardcover edition December 2021

Book design by Patricia Sparks
Illustrations by Patricia Sparks

ISBN 978-1-777-9875-2-7 (paperback)
ISBN 978-1-777-9875-1-0 (hardcover)
ISBN 978-1-777-9875-3-4 (ebook)

www.jenellesimpson.com

To all the people who have helped me step into my purpose, whether good or bad, I appreciate you dearly.

I don't believe that we meet people by accident or we are faced with certain situations for no valid reason, but there is a purpose in every person and situation.

To the loves of my life:

My circle of strong love and energy who always push me to dive deeper into who I am and my purpose.

My loyal backbones when I feel like mine is broken, who continue to extend and soak love and strength into me.

Laureen, my best friend and my "oh this is what authentic friendship feels like," thank you for that push I needed. Thanks for those words I needed to keep me going and stand solid in my purpose. Thanks for believing in me when I didn't believe in myself and being my voice and ear.

Love you unconditionally, I am proud and blessed to say, you are my best friend.

To my reason and eternal season:

Jason, Paula, Jo Jo, Daddy, Mommy, Holly, and Sweet, Sweet Grandma – you are all a part of me, a part of God's purpose in me and this book is dedicated to you. Your purpose is real, authentic, and God – given. It can never be stolen or replicated by anyone.

Rushawn and Laiyah, my babies and my greatest blessing in life, mommy loves you and don't let anyone change your hearts. You are full of purpose and your bond is perfect. God knew why he gave me two strong and perfect Lions.

JENELLE SIMPSON

To my soulmate:

Shane! My love, God was intentional about you and he knew what it would be TODAY.

You are my heartbeat, my best friend, my soulmate, and my forever. I love you and I pray that God continues to pour into and out of the both of us. Blessed to be connected to you and I pray God continues to cover our steps and strengthen our unity, parenthood, and purpose.

Our Journey has been and continues to be interesting and full of life and purpose.

You promised me love and never-ending change, you give me excitement to keep digging.
Love you always and for eternity.

Table of Contents

PREFACE vii

CHAPTER 1: Reliving 1

CHAPTER 2: Mawning Glory 7

CHAPTER 3: FML - F**K My Life 15

CHAPTER 4: Escape 23

CHAPTER 5: Sarah 30

CHAPTER 6: ADHD 33

CHAPTER 7: Dinner Chronicles 43

CHAPTER 8: Stolen Nights 45

CHAPTER 9: Instilled Fear 51

CHAPTER 10: Anthony 61

CHAPTER 11: Penetration 67

CHAPTER 12: Personality Shift 73

CHAPTER 13: Paradise 82

CHAPTER 14: Blame It On Voodoo 90

CHAPTER 15: Take Me Back 98

CHAPTER 16: Saturday 102

CHAPTER 17: Rooted Dysfunction... 107

CHAPTER 18: Don't Eat From People! 122

CHAPTER 19: Sunday.. 132

CHAPTER 20: Karma!.. 140

CHAPTER 21: Commitment To A Deceitful Liar 154

ACKNOWLEDGEMENT 165

AUTHOR BIO 168

Preface

When I was a kid, my desires were simple. I wanted to be successful, a lawyer, a strong voice within many communities, a writer, serve great purposes and help change the world. I wanted to be a singer, but I quickly accepted that I wasn't born with the gift of singing. I wanted four children with a heart so pure and loving, a strong, smart, determined, God-fearing, loving, hard, but gentle husband and a husband that had a heart – a big heart — for humanity and purpose. I wanted a big house that was a home, not just beautiful to the eyes, but a home that was warm and welcoming to all. I wanted a big, loving family that communicated, spent time, and loved together.

I wanted to build a separate home that would be a home for others who didn't have one, to help others and be that place where people of all walks of life could go and feel safe. I wanted to break generational cycles and break barriers people said weren't possible. Yet I also wanted to start and continue the good that our ancestors and the generations before us did. I wanted to be fearless and shift the generational tone. I told everyone I was going to be a lawyer and I was going to create my own home, community center, and shelter. Why? Because I love people and I wanted to make a big difference in the world that would continue for generations to come after me.

I was always a positive voice even when I was going through my own mess; I was always quiet, but my mind was always racing with a thousand words and thoughts of where I was going. I was very shy, but ambitious in what I wanted, and although it wasn't easy getting there and I stumbled along the way, I remained positive and believed that there was purpose in me. Even though I didn't quite see it at first, it was rooted in my heart and I had to dig it out. I quickly learned that life isn't always a straight line; we go through different seasons for a reason and everything we face in life is preparation for our next season. I learned that although we create a certain plan and life for ourselves, in my mind, if it's not aligned with God's plans for our lives, he will reroute us on his path. We have to learn to trust his guidance wholeheartedly even when we don't understand or see the entire road map. My plans were his plans, but not the same route I imagined.

So far in my life, I've been a paralegal. I am a Senior Law Clerk and co-owner (with my older brother and sister-in-law) of a non-profit organization that helps people, especially youths, find their way through life, providing food and financial support and so much more to a variety of people. Now I am really diving into my purpose with this book, my first book, trusting God and not resisting his instructions. "Commitment To A Deceitful Liar" first came from the shock and pain I felt from a deeply personal experience. In the moment, I felt numb, because I had never experienced going through such pain from someone who promised to love and protect me. This was someone who knew about my past traumas. But it was not a place that I was going to linger, and I got the urge to write books and use my experiences and journeys through life. I didn't believe I was the only person going through things in life, feeling stuck and not knowing how to start my healing process and allow myself to blossom out of my storms. I wanted to use my words and experiences to cause a shift in people and open them up. The title today serves as much more than one life incident – an inclusive umbrella of sorts. Lies come from many different sources throughout our lives. They can be dangerous. Once we begin unraveling those lies for answers, we don't always like what we find. But, through truth, we learn to forgive and create our own walk through life, not in the eyes of others, but our own and truly heal.

I pray that this book connects with you and opens an embracing self-love and new journey for you. We must accept our different journeys through life and embrace who we are; our experiences allow us to flourish through our healing. I pray for healing, love, and purpose in your life. Embrace who you are, and your experiences; take your time with yourself to heal and blossom.

Human Thoughts/Human Feelings/Human Stages

"Normalize going through and pulling through hard times. Normalize trying new approaches! Normalize learning new things! Normalize learning from people, admitting that you don't know everything and growing together is powerful! Normalize saying 'it's okay, I don't mind re-learning' and take time with yourself as you go through stages."

— Jenelle Simpson

Note To You, Yes you!

I believe that we can make real generational change and cause a shift if we truly believe in our own strengths and apply what God has given us. Dig deep and pull out all that stuff God has equipped you with and make the shift; you are overqualified and the perfect fit.

Sincerely, I believe and know you can.

CHAPTER 1

∽

Reliving

"Don't miss the signs and lessons because you're trying to travel too fast; enjoy each season, soak up everything, embrace and inhale life."

– Jenelle Simpson

I can feel a throbbing sensation; something doesn't feel right. The more we walk, the more I feel it penetrating me. Maybe I'm over exaggerating? Dah well, I'm almost at school. Finally, I arrive. I jump down quickly from his arms, so excited to see my friends I don't even say goodbye to my Uncle Mandela. My heart is racing and I'm feeling a little scared.

2:30 pm! Wow, that came around quick!

My grandma, whom we nicknamed "Sweetie," because she is as tiny and sweet as a candy, came and picked me up from school. Grandma has the most contagious personality — she is so cute, even her laugh, full of life with a big personality to match. Sweetie is more like my mother, as we have a close relationship and I know she loves me; I can see it in her eyes and feel it in her smile. I am her little mini-me, and she takes me everywhere with her. I wash clothes with her — she washes all our clothes with her hands, piece by piece, and I get to help. I think I can wash clothes well, but some would say I'm just playing with the clothes. My grandma is so smart, petite, strong, and beautiful. I just love her to pieces.

"MAMA Sweetie, what did you cook?" I yelled as I jumped up on her and she raised me up with her beautiful smile and glowing, small oval-shaped eyes.

"Not even a 'Good evening, Grandma?' How was school?" she replied.

"Mama Sweetie, school was alright, weh yuh cook, what did you cook?"

"I have to bring some food for Daddy lata, so, tell me what you cooked," I replied.

I was so excited to leave school and go home to see Grandma and eat her finger-licking delicious dinner.

Grandma can throw down in the kitchen. She loves cooking and that makes the food taste even better, all the love she puts in the food and time to make sure that we enjoy every bite. And I mean finger-licking, plate clean and nothing left behind.

"Likkle pickney stop nuh, mi cook likkle rice and chicken," Sweetie replied.

"Yes! Mi know wah dat means," I whispered to myself with excitement because I knew exactly what that meant.

She cooked chicken back (the back part of the chicken, yes!) and rice, one of my favorite meals mmmmmmm yum. I enjoyed chewing on the bones, sucking out the rich gravy juices dripping from them, and spitting the bones out. Grandma's gravy always tasted like some magical potion.

We walked home; it wasn't too far. My grandma gave me a quick bath, and I ate dinner and quickly prepared for bed. I didn't want to waste any more time being awake. I reminded Sweetie to make sure that she hid the food I left over for my daddy, and I would give it to him tomorrow or else, "dawg nyam yuh suppa." (If I'm not careful with what I have, I will lose it to someone else.)

I know my consequence will be someone in the house eating the leftover food I put aside for my dad and then later saying they didn't know it was for someone else.

I wouldn't want this to happen again, so this time I'm making sure Grandma helps me secure it by hiding it somewhere no one will be able to find it. *Craven retches*, they were all greedy and enjoyed the pleasure of eating someone else's leftover food.

I can't wait till tomorrow to see my dad because I haven't seen him in a while. My Aunty Kim, Grandma, and I all share one room and one bed, but it's very cozy. I feel safe and extra love sleeping beside my aunty and granny. I don't know what it feels like to have my own room and bed, but I certainly don't mind sharing.

We weren't a rich family; we lived in a small country, a bush area called Browns Hall in St. Catherine, Jamaica on top of a hill. The roadside and our house were at the bottom of the hill. We had to walk down a little alleyway in the front of the house to get to our house and we could hear all the cars passing by, all the honking, loud talking, and lots of music vibrating and beating throughout the Jamaican streets. Music is Jamaica's signature; it's our brand and identity. Music is tied to our culture, and it moves within our lives in so many significant ways. No matter what our circumstances are, music is our outlet.

The streets are loud. You can even hear people's personal business "ah roadside." We can hear everything about a person's life on the streets of Browns Hall. Our house is kind of hidden away and surrounded by bushes. You have to go around a big roundabout, up a long hill road, down, up, and all around to get to our house. The roads aren't the greatest either, lots of potholes and dips, but the drivers and pedestrians know how to handle the roads, because they are used to it. Granny would say, "Road dem bod, tek time nuh." She always expressed how bad the roads were, that the government needs to invest in fixing the roads and the drivers need to be careful when driving and stop being such aggressive drivers.

The streets are loud and filled with people. Everyone knows each other in our little bush community, and we are all like one big "likkle" family. There is no need for newspaper or television, as anything you want to hear someone will be able to tell all – "If ah nuh suh it guh ah suh dem seh it guh." Even if the story isn't true or exactly spot on, people will tell you that it's 100% percent true and they know this for a fact as if they had actually been there and witnessed it themselves. Everyone knows everyone's business; you can even hear people's personal business "ah roadside" -- everything about a person's life on the streets of Browns Hall. Everyone has "carry go bring come" to tell you, all you have to do is walk down the street and someone will tell you the latest and hottest gossip and story that's happening. Jamaicans always have some hearsay story, rumors, or private affairs of others to tell you that they heard from a friend of a friend, and it was so juicy they have to continue spreading it. You may even run into someone who can tell you all your own business you don't even know yet. Although our community loves to talk a lot and be all in the mix, we are very close, and not one of grandma's kids or grandchildren can do anything or behave in a way that doesn't represent Sweetie and she doesn't find out. Grandma always hears what happens before we even reach home to tell her, and she's already prepared to discipline us. Grandma would say, "Bend a tree while it is young, because when it is old it will break." Sweetie believes that children should be disciplined; teach them the right way when they are young, because trying to do it when they are older might be too late for them and yourself. And trust me, she was not afraid to grab a stick — or anything at that — to correct us and make sure we understood what we did was wrong.

Sweetie's house is the one everyone can come to and beg for sugar, water, and food — anything you need, Sweetie gives it with an open heart. Grandma has a big and caring heart. She is not mean and believes that even if it's your last bit of something, you must share it in as many ways as possible.

Everyone in the community knows Grandma and calls her Ms. Sweetie, and they know not to mess with her children or grandchildren.

She is always ready and prepared to fight for all of her children, especially my mom, and even when they were wrong, she was still fighting on the battlefield for them.

Sweetie turns on her gospel song so we can all fall asleep.

"I must tell Jesus

All of my trials

I cannot bear these burdens alone

In my distress

He kindly will help me

He ever cares and loves His own

I must tell Jesus."

(E. A. Hoffman (1894))

This is one of Grandma's favorite songs. She plays a lot of gospel music and if she can she'll "skank to the riddim." Grandma knows how to dance to the rhythm of any music beat and she is very good at it, too. Hmmm, maybe that's where I get my dancing skills from.

Faith is something Grandma Sweetie is very strict about, and she instills it in us daily. She reads her Bible every night; evening and morning, she is all about faith and God. She makes sure we don't forget to give God thanks and prays over each and every one of us as we go out, come in, wake up, and before we sleep.

Sweetie is crazy about "her" Jesus and her faith which no one could break. She makes it her business to make sure we understand the power of prayer and never forget to pray and trust God with and in everything we do.

No matter what the situation is or what circumstances come her way, she always keeps her faith running and she has a big backup generator to empower herself and everyone else.

Sweetie's faith is so strong, we would see her running "duppy" and pleading the blood against evil spirits all around the house, and she would have the Holy Ghost. She is fearless in spirit and in the natural. Grandma would be chasing ghosts away out of the house and around the house, under the anointing, and reading Bible Scriptures all around the house. Grandma don't play about her God and protecting her family.

Even when Grandma has problems, she's still telling everyone about the goodness of God and how wonderful God is. She never fails in her teachings and reminds us to give thanks for what we have, because things could be worse. Sweetie's favorite thing to say: "I am blessed, I am blessed every day of my life, I am blessed." Blessed and highly favored indeed we are.

CHAPTER 2

Mawning Glory

"You don't have to be religious to get to know God for yourself. Faith and God's love aren't contingent on your religion or the way you communicate with God. Don't let anyone stronghold God for themselves and force you to believe that God is not accepting of someone like you. Take your time, at your own pace and get to know God for yourself and not only through the mouths of other people."

— Jenelle Simpson

"Cockodoodle dooo dooo!" We live in the rural countryside of Jamaica so we are awakened daily by the roosters crowing all around the community. Every morning our roosters wake the whole house by approximately 5:00 a.m. They are so loud, I bet they are also the alarm clock for the entire community. It's like a piece of music that makes sure no one is sleeping in bed late; it's almost as if they crow until they sense that everyone is awake, up, ready, and moving about. We're so used to the rooster waking us up that our bodies are naturally programmed to wake up and get our day going.

The roosters crowing sound like music to our ears; I love hearing them in the morning and it really makes me feel happy to wake up freely to a "pleasant Jamaican mawnin."

Waking up in Jamaica is like waking up in paradise with true beauty soaking on our skins in the sunrise and the morning breeze breathing through our bodies. The fresh air feels soooooo good and soothing to wake up and start the day. Seeing everyone so happy and refreshed is priceless; the beautiful warmth and smiles on their faces give me peace. Everyone says "howdy" to each other. Even if they don't like you or know you, it's the Jamaican etiquette and manners to greet everyone and anyone. Everyone makes sure when they see each other to greet them with a smile on their face even if they are not happy, or do not know or like the person. The simple things are such a huge blessing.

"You don't have to like or know someone personally to show respect and love. Learn how to get out of your feelings regardless of what the circumstances are and be a daily reminder for someone else to keep going and smile through it. A smile and a small phrase can cheer a person all the way up and change the outcome of their day. Give a simple blessing of a smile or a hello."

- Jenelle Simpson

Everyone in Jamaica wakes up early. I don't think anyone sleeps beyond 8:00 a.m., because their day starts early and ends early. Kids get up early for school, adults get ready to go to work whether it's to go to the market, their 9 to 5, or to bush to plant ground and pick harvest to eat and/or sell at the market, and some just have their daily routine and wake up bright and early to go on the road and do road… "hold a medz, beat two juice" and listen to some music. Even if the person doesn't have a place of employment, they have a side hustle, whether that is selling second-hand goods or going to the farm to pick harvest to sell, and some just go on the road to hang out and chitchat with friends and family.

Jamaicans don't support laziness and believe that even if you don't have a job to go to or anything to do, you must wake up early and not sleep in bed. Sweetie and my dad would both say, "If yuh sleep ina bed all day, it will mek yuh big and wutless. Early to bed and early to rise, makes Jack and his master simple and wise." Dad believes that no one should be just laying around in bed doing nothing and you should go and find some type of hustle to do and not be lazy and worthless. The earlier you wake up, the luckier you will be.

Grandma Sweetie raises chickens and sells them to make money to take care of all of her children and grandchildren (my brother Anthony and me). I don't know how she does it all by herself with no man around the house to help other than her sons, no husband, and she's such a tiny woman, yet so strong and brave. Sweetie is so fearless I don't even know how it's possible. Grandma has ten children in total, five girls and five boys, but not all of them have the same fathers. Yet I've never seen Grandma with a man, just her, her children, and grandkids. Oh, and my dad plays a big role in Grandma's life and her children's. I always did wonder why Grandma had so many different babyfathers and why she never got married or stayed with any of them. I know there's nothing wrong with her, I mean she's beautiful, kind and so sweet, so what was the problem? Why did she go from one to the next? If I'm correct, I believe she has eight different babyfathers, but I don't know. Everything seems to always be a secret or none of my business because I am a child.

I wonder if she doesn't feel lonely at times. Her children who are overseas do support her a lot, sending her money and barrels with food, clothes, and other essential items, so she doesn't have to work much to make money. Sweetie just doesn't want to pressure her kids to always send stuff for her and she's just way too independent, but they do it anyways even without her knowing. Grandma doesn't and can't just sit around not doing anything; she's always on the go, go, go.

She chops off the chicken's head like a real slaughterhouse. "Yuck!" I whisper softly to myself.

Grandma Sweetie is a really strong woman, which can be seen in the way she uses the machete, the way she chops the chicken, and the way she does the yard work like a real boss woman. I know I am going to be just like my grandma when I am older. She takes really good care of me and always compliments me.

I just love my granny nanny and I can't imagine life without her.

I'm so excited to go to school today, because Sweetie will be walking me and then I'll be going to see my Daddio right after school.

"Boyakka!" I shout with joy as I twirled my itty-bitty waistline to the music beating down the street. Music is my favorite and dancing runs through my veins. I don't think I know how to stand or sit still when I hear music … the bass just beats through my body and gives me a loud vibe that makes me feel happy inside and all through my bones.

Can you hear and feel the music, the different beats that flow through one reggae song? Even if you can't dance, you just can't help yourself but to just rock away. Dance to the rhythm and enjoy the sweet melodies.

Everywhere you turn you hear the sweet island vibes; this little island is full of vibes, energy, and one love.

Sweetie made cornmeal porridge with a side of water crackers, yummy, one of my favorite porridges. These are my favorite hard crackers that have no real flavor but taste so good when crushed up into crumbled pieces and mixed all into my porridge. It is more filling and a better texture that way.

When there's not much to eat, Grandma makes it seem like a whole lot of food to share amongst us all, and trust me it took a lot to share among us all.

COMMITMENT TO A DECEITFUL LIAR

I ate my breakfast so fast I burnt the back corner of my tongue, but I didn't care. I was overly excited and I got dressed in my school uniform within seconds. I already wanted the day to end so I could see my daddy. Grandma Sweetie usually helps me get dressed, but she allows me to be independent and do things on my own, sometimes. She babies me, but not completely.

I see my dad whenever I want and mostly everyday. I live with Grandma Sweetie for the most part, and my dad lives at his own house not too far from Sweetie's house, but Anthony and I always go to Dad's house to spend time with him. It feels like I haven't seen him in months, but it has only been a few days, so you can imagine my anxiousness to see him. Dad is my favorite guy and he's perfect. I just couldn't wait to go to the shop with him, buy sweets, Cheecheks, and bag juice, and listen to music. Cheecheks are my favorite cheese sticks chips, kind of like Cheetos, and bag juice is juice in a bag that I just suck up and it tastes sooo yummy-ummy.

Thinking of Dad also brings up thoughts about Mom, who had left us and gone to Toronto, Ontario, Canada to work so she can create a better life for us all — Dad, Anthony, and me. Her plan is to work, save money, get her papers (Canadian citizenship) and then send for my brother, Dad, and me. She went to a foreign country without legal papers; I'm not sure about the details of that, but I know that she's not landed. She has no documents to show that she is allowed to be in Canada, but she sacrificed and took the risk for us. That was an opportunity Mom wouldn't pass up. Even if it meant her risking her life so we could have a better one, she did it and I'm sure she made the right choice which she felt would be best for us all. She works under the table and is living at Grandma's brother's house until things get better for her. I don't know how Mom got the opportunity to go to Canada, but she grabbed up that opportunity and left me with my grandma and dad to take care of me. I don't really remember spending much time with my mom before she left, but I miss her, and I talk to her on the phone almost every day. I know she loves me, but I barely know her.

I'm an old soul like my dad; I love to kick back, listen to some reggae music, and hang out at the shop.

"Mama Sweetie! Mama Sweetie! Mama Mama! I'm ready for school hurry up!" I scream out to Sweetie with my squeaky, cute voice.

I hear our dogs barking, so I turn my head quickly; they do this when someone is nearby or approaching the house. I see Uncle Mandela walking up to the front porch with a warped smile. He teases our dog by whistling and hails grandma.

"Good mawning, Mama Sweetie, how yuh doing? Mi will walk Danielle to school fi yuh," he said to Sweetie with a deep manly voice.

He smiled at me with his eyes, and I felt emotionless as he lifted me up in his arms. He wrapped my legs around his waist and threw my backpack over his shoulder.

"Thank yuh Mandela, now mi cyaan guh deal wid dem chicken and see weh mi cyaan sell ah market," Sweetie responded to Uncle Mandela.

It is warm today, and my heart is beating fast with suspense, but I don't understand why. He pulled my small waist closer and tighter around him each step he took. I felt a hard pressure on my "safety spot." His hands move down and tight under my tush. I've never felt this way before. I wiggle my way out of his hands with force and jump down running.

"Uncle! Come, I'll race you to school!" I yell out to Uncle Mandela as I run.

"Yuh sure yuh nuh wan me carry you, Danielle?" Uncle Mandela asked in a stern voice.

His voice is very deep; it sounds like there's bass coming out of his mouth; he could probably be a DJ if he wanted to with that deep voice.

"Noooo, I want to run so I can practice for when I become a track star....come run wid mi nuh," I respond with an unsteady voice in fear that he will be mad.

"Ouch!" I scream as I stumble, and I fall on the ground.

I had tripped and stepped on something sharp. It feels like something pierced through my foot.

With tears running down my face, I realize the bottom of my foot is bleeding. There he comes rushing over to me with suspense in his eyes.

"DANIELLE!" He yells my name as he rushes over to me.

He bends down, lifts my left foot, and there is blood flowing down my leg. A piece of hard metal had gone right into the side of the bottom of my left foot. He removes the piece of metal from the bottom of my shoe, takes off my shoe, and uses his shirt to wipe my blood from my foot. The cut wasn't as bad as it felt, only the blood looked scary, but, "I am fine, I am strong just like my grandma."

It felt awkward, him touching my foot, and I really didn't want him to do it anymore.

"Yuh okay, yuh wanna go back home and stay home with Sweetie today?" Uncle Mandela questioned.

"No, mi fine and I want to go to school today," I responded.

Again, he picks me up to carry me around his waist, but I stop him quick.

"Uncle, can I have a jockey ride?" (A piggyback ride is what you might call it.)

"Yes," Uncle Mandela responds with disappointment weighing on his face as he kneels down and I jump up on his back.

Beep beep beep, my alarm clock......ugh what a horrible dream, what kind of nightmare is this? And who is "Uncle Mandela"?

A figment of my imagination? Or did this really happen? My mom warned me about eating late in the night. She said I would have nightmares and see duppy, a ghost, late in the night. Jamaican myths! Ugh! 7:45 a.m., time to get ready for school. OMG! I'm going to be late for school and Mom is going to kill me. I can already hear her marching upstairs and cursing me out this morning. I better be quick and get ready....

Maybe one day I will be able to figure out who this Mandela person is and share it with you guys, but right now I need to go get ready for school before Mom turns up on me. She can go from 1 to 10,000 really quickly, mad woman.

"Dreams don't always walk straight, but there are some truths to our dreams, some of which are worth investigating and some are best left alone. Some nightmares are triggered by current events in our lives that cause us to relive a traumatic event we blocked out."

— Jenelle Simpson

CHAPTER 3

FML - F**K My Life

"Nip it in the bud; don't let it progress and turn into a bad habit. You have the ability to control how things repeat, replay, progress, and persist in your life; take that control and use it. You have the power and the resources to change things; use it and stop sitting in complaint."

— Jenelle Simpson

I hope he's not awake, because I can't stand him. The way he looks at me makes me feel naked and ashamed of myself. I feel so ugly and disgusted to be in my own skin and confused about who I am. He makes me hate the way I look. I slowly get out of bed, gently place my feet on the floor so the floors don't squeak … GOSH! I hate tiptoeing around the house! I feel like a stranger in my own house; I mean, I don't own the house, but it's my mom's house and I think I should be happy and feel free living here — and I don't.

Old houses. The floors are screeching as I walk towards my door. I whispered softly to myself with my eyes closed, "Please don't let him hear me."

I turned the doorknob sluggishly and pulled the door open gently, rushing quietly on my tippy toes to the bathroom and shutting the door.

Phew! His door is closed; he's not awake. I rush to get ready, wash my face, brush my teeth, and jump in the shower.

Uncle Ricky is my mom's younger brother. I don't know his exact age, but I know he is way older than I and he is a full-grown man. He came to live with us when he got arrested and my mom, my Aunty Beverly, and my Aunty Korraine had bailed him out of jail. All three of them had to come together to be his surety. Because of the type of charges and the severity, they had to show the court that they were good for the amount of the bail, and show that they had assets and the ability to supervise Uncle Ricky. There were a whole bunch of requirements I know nothing about and I only heard bits and pieces of the story.

One of his bail conditions is that he has to live with his surety, being my mom or one of her two sisters, and since all three sisters live in different homes, they all agreed that he could come live with us, because there's more space at our house for him and he would be able to have his own bedroom and be comfortable. Mom agreed, but she was not happy at all, and not because she didn't want to help her brother, but because she knew how her partner felt about her family. Mom and her partner, Uncle Tony, argued about Uncle Ricky coming to live with us for a long time, and Uncle Tony did not want him to come live with us, but Mom was already the bad apple and didn't want her family to dislike her more than they already did. So, she gave in and played the role of the good and supportive sister. Uncle Tony was not pleased with Mom's decision, because he hates our family and has worked overtime to divide and separate Mom from her family, especially her mother and siblings. He is very strong and robust with Mom, very harsh towards her, and I swear I don't even know what she sees in this cheesy-foot-smelling man.

Uncle Ricky had moved to Canada not that long ago and he had already found himself in trouble with the law—what a great newcomer's gift. Uncle Ricky came to Canada with Grandma Sweetie, Uncle Kenroy, and Aunty Kim. They all were sponsored by Aunty Beverly and Aunty Korraine to come to Canada, but Mom didn't help with this at all. I'm not sure why, but I know that her name was not on the sponsorship papers.

Mom and her sisters argued about this from time to time. Aunty Beverly and Aunty Korraine always made it a point to remind mom that she hadn't help with the sponsorship.

I think Mom only agreed to help bail out Uncle Ricky and allow him to come live with us as a way to make up for her past mistakes with Uncle Tony, and to get back in her family's good graces. Basically, she was using Uncle Ricky as a reason for her and her family to have a connection still through their brother. Our family has some deep-rooted issues that none of them seem to be in a hurry to solve, but Mom really just wants to be the savior and earn her way back into their hearts, which seems to be a very hard thing to do with people who are stubborn and stuck in their ways.

"You can't force your way back into someone's life or buy their forgiveness; you have to allow people to make their own decisions and pray for the best. Live your life and give people the space that they need to deal with their emotions their way, not your way."

— Jenelle Simpson

When Sweetie finally came to Canada to live, I was so excited. I finally got my mommy back and I felt like a new person; I was smiling from ear to ear. I used to spend every weekend with her and my cousins, and it felt almost the same as when I was a kid in Jamaica. I would have fun with Uncle Kenroy, Aunty Kim, and Uncle Ricky, believe it or not. I don't even know what changed. Why the sudden interest in me when he came to live with us? Did something change about me, and was I at fault in any way? Did I cause this to come onto myself? I didn't know what I had done, but I must have done something wrong.

Uncle Tony was the wedge that changed everything that I was dreaming of. I wanted my grandma to come and stay with me and when she finally did, Uncle Tony took that away from me. He stopped us from spending weekends with Sweetie and our aunties. Life just became darker and darker now that Uncle Tony was in our lives and there's nothing that Mom was doing to make Anthony and I feel any better. She just gave into him and gave all of herself to him, leaving nothing for Anthony and me. She hadn't even given that much effort to my dad. How could she be so selfish and not even think about Anthony and me first? What about our happiness?

I couldn't wait to grow up and have my kids — the love I am going to pour into them will be unbreakable.

I finished taking my shower very quietly and quickly.

I jumped out of the shower so anxious, wrapped my towel around me, and headed into my room so fast I forgot to breathe.

I wanted to be out of the house before he got up for work and saw me. My heart was racing in fear that I'd get caught.

My mom was downstairs; I could smell the oatmeal porridge she was making for breakfast. Barf! The smell was so heavy and just icky to me, and I couldn't see myself getting used to the smell.

I hate oatmeal porridge, but I knew I'd have to eat it. Mom doesn't care if you like the food or not, but you're going to sit and eat it or go hungry and/or get beatings from her "man." Mom allows Uncle Tony to beat us whenever and however. Mom only makes different foods for Ricky since he doesn't really eat meat.

I opened my drawer, took out my underwear, and threw it on vigorously along with my T-shirt and skirt mom had left on my bed for me to put on.

Yes, yes, my mom still picks my clothes out for me, and I am very annoyed, but what can I do? She buys the clothes, and I am still a child—in my mom's words. Do as you're told, wear what you're told, and eat what you are given.

> "Understood, parents are the caretakers and first road map for their children, and children must obey their parents' rules; however, parents should give their children the opportunity to uniquely have a choice to be themselves. Allow the person they were created to be to come out without forcing them to be someone you want them to be. Guide your children in the best way you know how, give them the necessities to go through and be successful in life, but don't force your beliefs, lifestyle, and clothing choices onto them; give them a choice to live, learn, and grow into their unique selves."
>
> –Jenelle Simpson

My door opened, and it was him, of course! My head started pounding and I was as scared as if it was a police officer beating at the door, just like when the police show up when Uncle Tony and Mom are fighting. My heart was racing as fast as the horses at the Woodbine racetrack, and I clenched my fists as tightly as I could, trying to make myself appear strong to myself.

What does he want? I think.

Uncle Ricky closed the door behind him, walked over to me like a slithering snake, and whispered in my ear, "Do you remember?"

He squeezed my right forearm, pulled me inwards, and stared at me with his egg-shaped, crooked, jaundiced eyes. His lips were so big and dark red; he looked so gross with the large gap between his front two top teeth.

He always smiles with it showing, but I'm not sure who told him it looked good, because it doesn't.

I yelled in a soft voice, "Stop it, your breath stinks and you're hurting me!"

I pushed him back and tussled with him, trying to get the door open. The door opens and he shuts it back. I dragged the door open a bit again and he slammed it so hard he got scared and released his hand from the door in fear that Mom heard the door slam.

I pulled the door open, rushed out of my room and headed straight downstairs to the kitchen. My heart was racing so fast I didn't even feel the rhythm anymore … feels as if I am the walking dead.

I'm surprised no one heard me because I felt like I was screaming at the top of my lungs, or at least my insides felt like I was screaming out to the world.

I wanted him to leave me alone. He's like a raccoon that keeps coming back late at night for garbage and I am apparently the garbage.

"Good morning, Mom, good morning, Uncle Tony," I said with a cheerful, but sarcastic voice.

Uncle Tony, to be clear, is my mom's boyfriend of approximately five-and-a-half years, well common-law partner to be correct, and I call him "Uncle" Tony, because mom told Anthony and me that's what we should call him. I can't stand him and the things he has done to us. He is the worst choice Mom has ever made in her life.

Funny enough, she even introduced him to Anthony and me as our "uncle," but we knew damn well he wasn't no uncle of ours. That was one of the biggest and most inappropriate lies she had told us. At first, I didn't realize it, but as I got older and saw how close they were, the late-night sleepovers, the noise in the bedroom, the amount of time he spent doing things that brothers and sisters should not be doing, I realized that she was a damn liar and a sick one.

She never even gave us a heads up or told us she was dating, but as a matter of fact, how could she? She was busy cheating on my dad, so why would she own up to that? My dad had been good to her, and she repaid him with evil, threw him out in the cold, and just left him for a complete stranger. She and Tony both treated my dad very poorly.

I assume she wants us to call him Uncle Tony out of respect instead of using just his first name or calling him "Dad." Which I guess is better because this man could never be my relative, but we could address him as "Mr. Tony."

He could never be my dad; my dad is human, and Tony, Uncle Tony, is something that appears to be human, but is really an animal. He doesn't even treat us like we're his children, but more like things he can boss around and control.

The tone and the way he treats us are weird; he even tries to tell my mom not to buy things for my brother and me, and when she does it's a big argument. Not sure why, but dah well we don't really care what he says.

Sometimes it feels like he doesn't like my brother and he is smartly competing with him. If Mom does something for Anthony, he has an issue and a mouthful to say.

Uncle Tony doesn't even do anything for his own children. He has three boys from his ex-common-law partner — Jamar, Iverson, and Chase. I overheard a heated conversation between Mom and him one day, that he doesn't even pay child support, and he and his babymother don't even speak; she despises him. Uncle Tony's babymother and my mom got into a physical fight when we used to live in Scarborough and the police were involved. I don't remember much about it, but I know it was late in the night; she left Anthony and me at home alone, and she and Uncle Tony were fighting—physically fighting—and it was pretty bad to the point the police were involved and Mom was physically hurt.

His sons don't want anything to do with him; he doesn't even spend time with them or bring them over for the weekend. What makes it even worse is the fact that Mom decided to have a child with him, our little sister Krystal, and that was the icing on the cake and the end game for Anthony and me. Her having a child with him and now having three kids just made things more official, and I can imagine how his kids feel; he just started a new family and forgot about them.

"Being a parent is more than just laying down rules, providing shelter, clothes and food, and stomping feet. Children require so much more from their guardian, a deeper connection and love. Being a step-parent requires work and patience; just because they're not your biological children doesn't mean that you should treat them differently and exclude them."

— Jenelle Simpson

CHAPTER 4

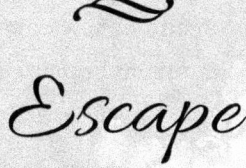

Escape

"Sometimes you gotta cuss people out in your head, not out loud, keep your pleasant smile, and keep it moving. Your silence is powerful, but that doesn't mean you don't have mental outbursts and that's NORMAL! Keep your peace, protect your peace, and learn not to entertain certain things and people that come with it."

– Jenelle Simpson

"**D**id you brush your teeth and wash your face?" Mom questioned.

"Yes, Mom! Can't you tell?" I responded with a bit of a tone underneath but tried to cover it with a smile and cuteness in my voice, so the attitude wasn't noticed.

"Ding dong, ding dong!" Saved by the bell, the doorbell rings.

It was my friend Sarah. It was really hard to make new friends when we moved here to Pickering, Ontario, but Sarah made it easier for me to blend in and feel comfortable.

We walked to school together every morning. She was my closest friend since we moved here, along with my other best friend, Tamar.

Tamar and I are much closer than Sarah and me; we are more like sisters, but we don't go to the same elementary school, so we mostly talk on the phone for hours when Mom and Uncle Tony aren't home. We try to enjoy the

minimal time that we get to see each other when Mom allows me to go to my friends' houses which is almost never. Mom can be so hypocritical, she doesn't want us to go to anyone's house, but yet she also doesn't want people at our house, however, she would rather us go to our friends' houses. She says she doesn't want any girl "pickney" around her son to tell lies that he touched or did something inappropriate to them. She claims to be protecting us, but I think this rule is because of Uncle Tony and then Mom's own personal experiences.

Mom has too many negative thoughts and theories; to me, she sounds crazy, but she says, "Children must obey and listen to their parents and who cyaan hear must feel." Mom always comes with a mouthful of lyrics to tell us that we should listen to our parents and if we don't something bad is going to happen to us. Blah blah blah blah, she goes on and on about the same things over and over again. We already know exactly what she is about to say without her actually opening her mouth.

Tamar and I share clothes, but Mom doesn't know because I hide the clothes that she gives to me somewhere in one of my drawers or closet where she won't be able to find them. Tamar's mom allows her to pick out her own clothes, and she wears more grown-up clothes like push-up bras, tube tops, and tight clothes. My mom is very strict about the way I dress, so she doesn't allow me to buy certain types of clothes.

Tamar gave me my first push-up bra, and she was the first friend to break me out and introduce me to the boyfriend topic. She has a boyfriend. I think she is too young, but her mom allows her to.

If Mom knew I was taking stuff from my friends she would cuss me out and tell me, "Bring it back." Mom emphasizes that we shouldn't take things from people, and we must be careful of friends.

She says "don't bring people's crosses things" in her house, "people might have put obeah in it" to tie me, hold me down, and/or hurt me in life. I must stop walking on the road and taking things from people, because people will take it and talk bad about me after. We must not trust everyone that "skin teeth with us." Mom has many interesting ways of making sure Anthony and I understood not to trust people and that not everyone that smiles with us is really our friend, basically emphasizing that most people, if not all people, are fake.

"Obeah" is a kind of sorcery practiced especially in the Caribbean and also known as witchcraft, black magic and/or voodoo.

The way Mom speaks seems to be from an experienced and hurt place as if she's gone through all these things and she's trying to protect us. But she doesn't realize that it's pushing us away and causing us to have deeper trust issues. I would say that I have major trust issues, but I don't plan to remain like this forever, and I will break this generational pattern, and not let it progress.

I do remember a story that has been floating around that a lady in Jamaica performed voodoo on mom. She and her mom sent a letter to my mom in Canada about my dad, telling my mom that she had been in a sexual relationship with my dad and my mom should leave him alone, and end their relationship. Apparently, when my mom opened the letter, it had some sort of oily substance on it. They say the oily substance caused Mom to go mad and confused and felt like there was a spirit on her that was trying to kill her. She even had to cut off all her hair, and Mom had long, natural, and beautiful hair. Mom was so sick, she had to call

Grandma Sweetie and she had to go to a special church to be prayed for and a whole bunch of mess. It was a big thing.

I don't think my dad really cheated on my mom, but that's another story to dive into later.

Mom tries to protect my brother and me at all costs; it doesn't matter what she has to do, she will do it.

"Mom, I have to go. Sarah is here and we're going to be late," I yelled out to mom.

"Wait, wait! Your breakfast…" Mom replied.

"Make sure you eat your breakfast and don't throw it away, DANIELLE," she said in a stern but funny voice.

"Yuh see yuh face, yuh ah jinal (trickster)," Mom said with a big smile on her face.

Mom has big, high, beautiful cheekbones and a million-dollar smile, and I guess that's where I get it from.

Funny how parents know their children and what we will do, because that is exactly what my plan was—to throw it away in one of the bushes on our way to school.

"I hate oatmeal porridge with all these added Jamaican spices," I mumbled back to my mom, but under my breath.

Mom goes overboard with flavoring her porridges, and some I like and some I can't even swallow, especially when she puts the nutmeg in it.

I grabbed the mug from her hand and quietly kissed my teeth out of frustration, not to disrespect her.

She kissed me on my cheek, put her hand on my head and said the Lord's Prayer:

> Our Father in heaven,
>
> hallowed be your name,
>
> your kingdom come,
>
> your will be done,

on earth as in heaven.

Give us today our daily bread.

Forgive us our sins as we forgive those who sin against us.

Save us from the time of trial, and deliver us from evil.

For the kingdom, the power, and the glory are yours,

now and forever.

Amen.

(Matthew 6:9-13)

She had a small bottle that looked like perfume. She opened the cap, placed her index finger over the hole, poured a tiny bit on her finger, and rubbed some behind both of my ears.

"Be safe, have a wonderful day, God bless you and I love you," Mom said.

I don't know how she has this faith, but still talks about obeah religiously. When I bring this up to my dad he gets upset and says, "Mi nuh wan hear bout dem flipping sumting deh, ah only God mi seh…yuh hear me."

Dad doesn't want to hear anything about no obeah, only God.

I opened the door and greeted Sarah with a flattering smile.

"Good morning, Sarah!" I said.

"Good morning, girl, let's go," Sarah replied with her big blue eyes wide open and her nose flaring.

"Good morning, Aunty Claudette," Sarah said to mom.

"Good morning honey, how are you?" Mom replied.

"Okay, you guys have a great day and Lala make sure you eat your breakfast!" Mom added.

I felt so relieved being out of that firewall we call a house. Any minute I could get out I really savored it and took my time, because once I got inside, I felt like I was in a prison cell.

Free from that environment, my mind started to wander." School and my friends are my escape room and I unleash all my beauty when I am around them. At school, I hold back my true self a lot out of fear and what they will say, but I still try to be free and laugh when I can.

I wondered what it would feel like to be in a real prison. Is the food good? *I think I would prefer to be in prison than live in this home,* I think to myself.

If I had to choose between home and prison, hmmm, believe it or not I'd choose that jail cell. I'd eat whatever they gave me just to be away from this toxic thing they refer to as a family and a home. This can't be normal at all, and I pray that I don't carry and transfer this lifestyle in my own life and to the family I will create for myself.

"Hey, who's that guy standing outside of your house?" Sarah questioned.

"It's my mom's brother, Ricky. He recently moved here from Jamaica with my other uncle, aunt, and my granny Sweetie. He's staying with us for a while," I replied.

"How comes I've never seen him before?? He looks kind of creepy the way he stares at me, but girl he fineeeeee!!! That's really your uncle? He looks kind of young," Sarah said in an awkward voice that seemed too weird for a 12-year-old to be using towards a grown man.

Sarah has way too many questions, and I don't have any answers for her.

I wasn't allowed to talk about boyfriends and girlfriends. Uncle Tony is very strict and has a good way of reminding me of what will happen if he hears me talking about boys or finds out I'm having sex.

He regularly says, "Nuh talking about nuh fucking boyfriend or girlfriend in yah." In his rough and loud voice, he made sure I knew that boyfriend and girlfriend topics were strictly off-topic and I should stick to schoolwork topics.

If there was an award for the person who spoke the best to children about this, he would win that a million times a million and die with the status and trophy.

I started singing a song by the Spice Girls, "Stop," to change the topic and prevent Sarah from asking more questions about that gully bop.

COMMITMENT TO A DECEITFUL LIAR

Sarah and I sang the rest of the way to school. We sang out loud at the top of our lungs with no care in the world. I tried to enjoy every moment being outside of my house, so I was always acting goofy and singing out loud.

I can't sing, I just wasn't blessed with that gift and it's so strange because I love to sing, and I love dancing even more. I did get the gift of dancing, though, and my dance moves are "bussn bussn."

We used to go to Aunty Korraine's house for entire weekends and have dance battles, and of course, I am the best dancer out of all of them. Music and my body have a natural connection and I just know how to rock with any beat.

Sometimes I dream about being a music video girl for a short period of time, but nah I know I'll be a lawyer and serving people all throughout the world.

"Singing is a language, you can feel a person's whole heartbeat through their music, their soul and intentions. Music speaks and heals; music is layered and tailored to move different emotions."

— Jenelle Simpson

"What you truly desire can become your reality with hard work, determination and patience. Just because your dreams don't happen on your timing doesn't mean they will never happen. If it's a part of God's plan for your life, best believe it will happen, even in the darkest moments of your life."

— Jenelle Simpson

CHAPTER 5

Sarah

"People may look at you and stare, they may even laugh, they may start whispering and attempt to make you feel uncomfortable but CHIN UP! You've got things to do, things to manifest, and levels to climb; don't get distracted."

— Jenelle Simpson

COMMITMENT TO A DECEITFUL LIAR

"Sarah, want to come over after school today? We can do homework and hang out for a bit," I said in a nervous voice, praying that she said yes.

"Yeah, sure!" she replied.

I should have asked Mom first before inviting a friend over, but meh it's not that big of a deal today. I just needed to make sure Sarah stays with me for a few hours as my distraction.

When we finally arrived at school, we could see all our other friends, Kimone, Trisha, Laureen, Dominique, Katerina, Stacey, and Lisa standing outside on the playground talking and laughing up a storm.

Sarah became awfully quiet as soon as we walked over to the school and approached our group of friends. Sarah was full of life, outgoing, and loud and I would say she is extremely fun. Some would disagree and call her annoying, but meh! Some were her friends and still laughed behind her back. What a bunch of cowards—mean girls and fake as *fakkk*.

Sarah made a lot of jokes, and she was the light in the room with her big voice. She had an "I don't give a shit" attitude, but I knew her beneath the tough exterior. I knew that she found ways to block out the negative energy people gave her and that gave me life to try my best to be myself and care zero what other people said or felt. She made me dig into my self-love a little more every time I saw the way she loved herself. She had power written all over her and in her presence.

I love Sarah, she is bold and brave …. nothing like me.

A lot of the kids torment Sarah about her weight and the large bump on the left side of her nose which makes her look a little different from everyone else. I personally think she's beautiful, made perfect, and unique, and believe me Sarah knows that she's beautiful; her confidence level is at A1. I strive to have confidence and heart like her. If self-love was a person, it would definitely be her.

They called her "marble nose." I like her nose although the other kids mock her daily and whisper when she passes. I don't care—she's my friend, my best friend, and I love her.

The school bell rings for us to go inside, and we all start walking towards the school.

Sarah and I stayed close together because we were in the same class. We headed to class and began our day with morning prayer.

3:30 p.m. came around quicker than I expected, and I didn't want to go home just yet.

"Ting ting ting!" The dismissal bell went off.

It's time to go home. I'm still sitting in my chair; I don't want to leave. I wish I could run away and move in with a new family.

"Hey Danielle, you ready?" Sarah asked.

Sarah's voice shocked me from behind and jolted me out of my daydream.

"Huh? Ready for what?" I questioned.

"Time to go home and remember, you invited me over," Sarah replied.

"Oh yes! Ok, let's go," I responded.

On our way to my house, we stopped at the convenience store to get some candy; both Sarah and I have a bad case of sweet tooth. We eat candy almost every day.

We bought some big lollipops that had bubble gum on the inside, which were my favorite type of candy.

We left the store excited with all our candy and started walking the long way around to my house, which takes us past Sarah's house. This was my idea so I had more time outside and with Sarah. The longer way wasn't much longer, but it was a small way to kill some time.

"Never focus on the chitchat and what everyone else around you is saying. Either they love you or they don't, not your concern. Stay true to who you are and the real friends around you, because authenticity is rare and good friends are hard to find."

-Jenelle Simpson

CHAPTER 6

ADHD

Pain/Trauma/Healing - I am Changing My Life Tone
"Stop making fun and passing judgement on pain you've never experienced. Extend love when you don't understand, not your knowledgeless and biased opinions."

— Jenelle Simpson

We finally arrived in front of my house, where we saw my new neighbor, who was tall, had caramel skin, had curly low-cut hair, and had a whole lot of looks going on.

"Hey, Kevin," I said with a soft and shy voice.

Kevin just moved here from Alberta with his mom and older brother.

He's a mixed breed, half black and white. He's thirteen years old and a few months older than I, but he has a mischievous smile .... oh, his smile makes you wonder what he's thinking and that he must be up to no good! And packaged with a mean temper.

Kevin has ADHD, attention deficit hyperactivity disorder, which would perhaps explain his bad temper and outbursts at times. ADHD is a "neurobehavioral condition." It makes it hard for someone to pay attention and to control impulses, but Mom and Uncle Tony make it seem as if Kevin is a bad child and having ADHD is a crime. They think he's sick and only because he's a mixed-up breed. I think they are crazy, and they think they know everything, but they don't. I don't think having ADHD is a crime or a bad thing. I've learned that many people have it and that doesn't mean that they should be labeled.

Mom and Uncle Tony always have their many opinions and beliefs.

> "When we don't understand things, we label it whatever we feel is personally fit, rather than educating ourselves and stepping outside of our personal knowledge. Step outside of your comfort knowledge and soak up new knowledge."
>
> – Jenelle Simpson

All of the girls at school think he's cute, even Sarah. She blushes every time she sees him, and her nose starts to flare up like a kid at the candy store, but not me.

I giggle.

I think he's cute, but I will never admit it.

Sarah shrieked with a flirty voice, "Hey Kevinnnnnn!"

Kevin turned and replied in a mimicking voice, "Hi Sarah," as he smirked.

Kevin was also one of the people who made fun of Sarah because of her appearance, but of course, he did it behind her back and in an interesting way, not disrespectfully, but enough to make me mad. I think Sarah knows, but it doesn't bother her; she still thinks he's cute and delicious (her words, not mine).

Sarah whispers to me with her fantasizing voice, "Mm mm, that boy is fine, I wish I lived next door to him."

We rushed inside my house, giggling loudly.

"Mom, Mom, I'm home and Sarah is with me. We're going to do homework together," I yelled out to Mom.

"Danielle," Mom replied in a firm voice.

"Yes, Mom," I replied.

She responds, "Come here," in her stern voice.

I ran into the kitchen and saw her making dinner. Mom loved cooking even when she was dead tired and not in the mood.

Mom's belief is that we have to eat full-blown meals every day and it supports our growth. Mom likes to remind me of how petite my body is and how short I am. She likes to convince herself that the more I eat, I'll just sprout up like a tree and put on some pounds.

Who knows, maybe she's right, but I think I was meant to be small and short like my dad. Mom is much taller and bigger in body; Dad seems to have a thing for women bigger than him.

> "Genetics play a big role in a child's features and body size and sometimes no amount of food or lesser food can change that. Some people are tall like giraffes, and some are short, because of their family genetics."
>
> — Jenelle Simpson

"Hey, Mom, is Krystal sleeping?" I said, trying to change the topic of her cussing me.

"No!" she replied with aggression.

I knew better, I knew the rules and these were rules followed and never disobeyed, but there has been a sudden shift in everything I do.

"Next time before you invite a friend over, come home first and ask me. You know the rules."

"Sorry, Mom," I responded, "but Sarah followed me, and I didn't want to be rude and tell her no, because her parents aren't home." Although I knew that wasn't true, I figured if I passed the blame onto Sarah, Mom wouldn't be so so mad at me, and she would just let it go this time.

Mom replied, "How was school?" and yelled, "Sarah, you want anything to drink, darling?"

"Yes, please," Sarah replied.

Sarah walked into the kitchen and Mom handed Sarah a glass of juice, "fruit punch," with a slice of bun and cheese. Mom didn't ask Sarah if she was hungry, but one of Mom's favorite things to do is feed people, especially our friends when they came by. Mom loves to share and give, give, give — she was a consistent giver.

Sarah liked this bun and cheese, as it's the Jamaican cheese that comes in the big can and oh boy, DELICIOUS.

COMMITMENT TO A DECEITFUL LIAR

We went upstairs. Although my mom has a "no friends upstairs and in the bedroom" rule, I still break it. We did our homework, watched TV, gossiped, and laughed.

"6:30 p.m. already!" Sarah said and jumped up.

She grabbed her workbook off the pink-carpeted living room floor and packed her bag in a rush. We have pink carpets, the Pepto-Bismol type of pink all on the stairs, upstairs, in the hallways, and in every bedroom. It's not a pretty color at all and I do not like it.

"I have to go home now. My dad will kill me if I'm not home before 7:00 p.m.," she said.

Sarah threw her backpack over her shoulder and rushed down the stairs.

"Bye, see you tomorrow at 8:15 a.m., girl," she said.

"Goodbye, Aunty Claudette, thanks for having me over, see ya!" Sarah yelled to my mom.

She calls my mom aunty — that's how close we are.

"Do you want me to walk you home?" I yelled back to her.

"No, it's okay, it's right around the corner. See you tomorrow!" Sarah responded.

"Okay, call me when you get home. Bye!" I yelled.

A bitter taste is in my mouth, my stomach feels empty, and I start to feel warm, starting from my head all the way down to my toes, as soon as it hit me that Sarah was gone.

Sarah is so different, she makes me wonder and question myself.

Sarah kissed me once on my lips and I still don't know what that was all about or how to feel about my own self. It didn't make me mad, but it made me question if Sarah liked girls……..wait! do I like girls?

"I hate him, I hate him," I whispered to myself. I wondered where my brother was. Oh, I forgot, he's staying at Aunty Korriane's house this week. Anthony sometimes stays at our Aunty Korraine's house because it's closer to his school and easier for him to get there in the mornings instead of taking multiple buses from our house to get there.

Anthony is four years older than me, he's in highschool and mom was very particular about what school she wanted him to attend – a Catholic School was crucial for her.

Mom sent him to St. Evans Catholic Secondary School, claiming it's one of the best schools within Durham Region and also because it's right down the street from Aunty Korraine's house.

I went upstairs and grabbed my baby sister out of her playpen.

"Hey princess, goochy goochyyyy." I tickled her and played with her fat tummy while she clenched onto me, smiling, with her bright brown eyes telling me to stop.

"Danielle, gwan go bathe and get ready to eat your dinner, yuh have school ina di mawning," Mom yelled.

"Mom, I'm not feeling well, I'm not hungry," I responded.

"Yuh want likkle peppermint tea?" Mom asked.

"NO!" I responded with irritation in my voice.

Geeze, more Jamaican myths!

Every time you say you don't feel well, they offer tea – peppermint tea, ginger tea, garlic tea, you name it they will offer it to you as a remedy even if you have a toothache, which rarely works ... NEVER WORKS!

I say to Mom, "My tooth hurts" and her response, "Drink some tea." I started laughing out loud to myself as if I'm a mad woman.

I put Krystal in her baby swing and walk to my bedroom. I could smell him; his smell lingers in the hallway, and I felt like I could just barf right here. I attached a mysterious smell to him.

I hadn't always felt this way about him; I actually used to like him, and I even told people that he was one of my favorite uncles. He used to be so fun and someone I didn't mind spending time with.

I closed my room door softly hoping he wouldn't hear me. He seems to be able to sense my presence and when I am home, waking up, or just anywhere at all. He must have a special sense just for me, because I don't know how he knows when I am here.

I grabbed my pajamas, head wrap, and underwear so I could get dressed in the bathroom. I heard a soft knock at my door.

I yelled, "Yes, who is it?" but no one answers. Instead, my door slowly opens. My heart is racing again. I knew it was him just by the way no one answered. If it were Mom, she would have yelled with her loud mouth.

He poked in his big head with low-cut hair and waves for days.

"When yuh finish bathe, come ina mi room," he said.

I grind my teeth and my body goes numb and I don't even have the guts to respond.

He stood there hunched over in between me and the door with a possessive look on his long, slender brown face.

What does he want from me, and why doesn't he just go back where he came from? I held my breath as he walked away and left my door. I slowly walked with my fist clenched so tight, I could feel my veins pulsing. His perfume or whatever the hell he was wearing reeked. He stood in the hallway and for the first time, he didn't reach for me or try to grab me. "Phew."

I paced into the bathroom and slammed the door. I slowly released my breath and took small breaths in and out to calm myself down from having a panic attack.

"DANIELLE!" Mom shouted.

I replied nervously, "Yes, Mom?"

"Don't slam my door like that," she replied.

I miserably respond, "Sorry Mom, it was an accident."

I let the water run for ten minutes and fill the tub to the top. I stare at the water flowing softly into the tub with tears rolling down my cheeks. "How did I get myself into this turmoil?"

It took me a whole forty-five minutes to bathe. I tried scrubbing it all off, but I can still see it. Why is it still there? The words on my face, the bruise on my arm from him squeezing and hitting me?

I dry myself with my towel, lotion my skin softly, admiring every inch of my body, wondering what it is about my small physique that could possibly attach someone to me. I gently take my time and put on my clothes in hopes that everyone would be asleep by the time I finish. Yeah right, Mom would never go to bed without coming to check on me and say goodnight. It was her nightly routine, and she has never missed a night even when she is in a bad mood and she and Uncle Tony had a fight.

Knock knock knock, there's a knock on the bathroom door. *Is it him? God! When will he stop?* I speak to my inner self.

Every time I'm in the bathroom he pretends he needs to use it or complains to Mom about me and tells her I'm taking too long and he needs to use the bathroom. I mean it's my house, so he can wait or go and use Mom's bathroom.

Mom yelled, "DANIELLE, open the bathroom door. Why would you be taking a shower so long, yuh crazy? You will make the wata bill high, have likkle consideration for me nuh. Yuh know seh mi try and a me one."

Mom always stressed that it was her alone that's doing things and paying bills. Which doesn't make much sense, because she has a man, Uncle Tony, and he's working, so how could it possibly be just her alone doing everything?

That would explain why Sweetie and the rest of the family call him "wutless" (worthless) and "Ms. Janey."

OH SHOOT!! It's my mom! Thank goodness.

"Okay Mom, I'm coming, almost done. Just getting dressed," I said with a frightened and worried voice.

I threw on my clothes quickly, opened the bathroom door, and there she stood staring with an angry face like a bull.

"Come downstairs and eat your dinner and then get prepared for bed," she said.

"Mom, I'm not that hungry and my stomach is still hurting. I just want to sleep," I replied.

Although my stomach wasn't hurting at all, I told a lie anyways because I wanted to be alone. I've also been trying to eat less so I would lose weight and I wouldn't look so "appealing" to the male eye.

> "People have different attractions and fetishes, some weird fetishes and some that appear to be normal to some. Some like big, some like small, some like soft, some like rough, some like tall, some like small and believe it or not, some are attracted to children. Be aware of the signs with people around your children."
>
> — Jenelle Simpson

"Come, I will make you some tea," she replied.

She wrapped her arm around my shoulder, and we walked downstairs to the kitchen.

"You must eat food so you will have a strong healthy body," she said.

Here she goes again talking about my body, my body!

I hate my body! My curves, my perfectly small, round-shaped buttocks, my new developing breasts, and my flat tight and firm stomach.

I'm annoyed. I hate it! She constantly talks about my figure.

I wish my body looked more like Sarah's; I wouldn't even be noticed. Sarah is bigger in body with no real shape, kind of like a barrel and I mean that with no disrespect whatsoever. I love her and there's nothing wrong with her body, but I would have preferred her body so I would go unnoticed.

"Self-hate stems from somewhere and someone. We don't just wake up and hate the texture of our hair, the shade of our skin, the shape of our features, but someone instilled something in us to cause that dislike and hate for self. Learn how to re-love yourself and don't allow anyone to define the way that you love yourself. Self-love will always be the best form of love. Sometimes we have to learn how to love ourselves again and block out the outside influences."

– Jenelle Simpson

CHAPTER 7

Dinner Chronicles

"Everyone's experience in life is different; what's painful to you may not be painful to them and that's not to be criticized."

– Jenelle Simpson

I headed down to the kitchen, sat on the chair, and he was sitting right across from me eating white rice, curry chicken, and a side of mixed vegetables. He ate as if he was just released from prison, where he belongs.

He looked up at me with his bottom lip droopy and his oval creepy jaundiced-looking eyes. He mumbled something to me under his disgusting breath, but I couldn't understand. I immediately held my head down. *I wish he would choke on a piece of chicken bone, dirty prick,* I think to myself.

"Mom, I don't want so much food, please," I said.

She shouted at me, "Shut up yuh mouth and eat the food!"

I angrily took the plate from her hand and my emotions sunk in my chest.

"You're always forcing me to eat," I murmured under my breath.

Mom yelled, "What did you say?"

I replied with a sarcastic smile, "Nothing."

I ate my dinner fast. I didn't even chew and I swallowed as fast as I could.

You know that feeling when you have tears overflowing on the inside of you and it's clogging your throat so that you can barely swallow? Well, that's the feeling I am experiencing.

I excused myself from the dinner table, emptied the remaining grains of rice left on the plate into the garbage bin, put the plate in the sink, and rushed upstairs to get ready for bed.

"Goodnight Mom and Uncle Tony," I said. I don't even bother saying goodnight to Uncle Ricky.

"Alright, goodnight," Mom and Uncle Tony respond at the same time.

I rushed upstairs, went into the bathroom, brushed my teeth twice as mom taught me, and off to bed I went.

Dinner has not been the same since uncle Ricky moved in. It's so strange how he terrorizes me with his eyes and I instantly lose my appetite.

CHAPTER 8

Stolen Nights

"Just because the trauma happened a long time ago doesn't mean the trauma isn't still there. Start talking about it and start your healing process; don't allow anyone to force you to forget and just 'get over it.'"

— Jenelle Simpson

I jumped in my bed and covered my head with my blanket. I was afraid of the dark, so I hid under my sheets; I have a night light, but that still doesn't help my fear.

Mom came upstairs. I could hear her talking and walking towards my bedroom door.

She opened my door and walked over to my bed, tiptoeing so she wouldn't wake me up if I was already asleep. She laid her hand on my forehead and prayed over me and finished with a kiss on my forehead.

"God bless you, love you," she said.

She drew the door up enough to leave a little crack so some light from the hallway could shine into my room. She knew I hated the dark and how afraid I was. She also hates when bedroom doors are closed. I think it's because of Uncle Tony because he said nobody should be in no room locked up.

The rules Uncle Tony enforces really don't even make much sense to me, but whatever — we listen, follow, and obey because we're afraid of him, mainly his strong and superior voice.

I fretfully struggle to fall asleep, waiting to hear if Uncle Ricky would come into my room. I wait a little bit every night to make sure he falls asleep before I do, because I know he won't come in here if my mom is still awake.

Mom usually stays up late to clean, get my school clothes prepared for the next day, and pack my lunch. When I was eleven years old, Mom used to make all of the decisions on what I would wear, and it always turned out to be dresses and skirts. Recently, now that I'm twelve-and-a-half, she lets me be more independent and decide what I want to wear most of the time. Oh, how I'm glad I don't have to wear bubbles and clips in my hair anymore. The boys at school used to call me "pineapple head," because my conrows stuck out like the stem of the pineapple every time mom would cornrow my hair.

I learned how to cornrow my own hair this year when Mom was frustrated with me after washing my hair. She argued with me about learning how to do my own hair, because I was old enough. I stood facing the big mirror on the wall and behind the couch and took my time learning the technique of mastering braiding my hair. That was the day I learned how to braid and style my own hair myself, and that's the day I was able to be unique and wear my hair how I chose to.

Mom also stays up waiting for Tony, oops I mean "Uncle Tony," to get home from work. I really don't like Uncle Tony's personality, because he makes my mom sad, and he's aggressive, obnoxious and abusive most of the time, mostly verbally abusive.

My mom is truly a SUPER WOMAN! She just keeps going and going like an Energizer battery.

I don't hear anything; the house is awfully quiet now. I know Uncle Tony is home, though, because I heard his big mouth enter the door, so it must be around midnight. I'm not sure what the time is because my head is still hiding under the sheets.

Okay, now I can go to sleep.

"Zzz Zzz Zzz Zzz Zzz Zzz - I can hear myself making snoring sounds.

Ahh not this dream! I'm having that dream from the other night. I know all my mom's siblings and she doesn't have a brother or cousin that I know of named, "Mandela."

I can see his face; he's walking towards my grandma's house with a smile on his face as if he is pleased to see me.

I feel a soft touch on my leg with a soft whisper by my ear, "Mi wan some." I smell morning breath.

I jumped out of my sleep, startled with fear. I took the sheet off of my head, looked up, and saw him hovering over me. He stared at me with an agonizing look on his face and his big nasty dark red lips drooping.

I have a bad feeling in the pit of my stomach, but my mouth is motionless — not a word I say. I feel like screaming, but instead, I finally say, "What?"

He repeated, "Mi wan some!" *What does he mean by "he wants some?" Some of what?* I think to myself.

I clenched my whole body tight and said nothing. Almost as if I am a frozen statue.

He whispered, "Do you remember when you came to Jamaica?"

I'm confused; I don't respond, and he grabbed my face to kiss my lips. I fold my lips shut so tight, both his bottom and top lips covered my whole mouth. His breath smells nasty, and now all his saliva is on my mouth and it smells like pooh.

I closed my eyes and remembered. We went to Jamaica last year when I was eleven years old for my great grandma's funeral, and it was around Christmas time. That was the first time I'd been back to Jamaica since I had moved to Canada in May 1995. I hadn't remembered him when I first saw him, but he definitely had remembered me. I left when I was very young, about five years old, so my memory is very unclear from when I was a child.

I barely remembered any of my family back home in Jamaica, but I can remember most of my aunts and uncles.

When he laid eyes on me, he stripped me with his eyes, and I'll never forget what he said. "You grew so big and sexy. Do you have a boyfriend? I want to be your boyfriend," he said to me.

I remember being afraid and not saying much. I asked him, "Are you not my uncle, how can you be my boyfriend?" But I don't remember his response.

He tried very hard to get me alone when I was visiting Jamaica, but my Aunty Kim took me everywhere with her as if she knew and she was protecting me. He also tried kissing me, but my grandma walked into the room just in time and he pulled away like a thief in the night.

I never stayed around him, and I would never stay in a room by myself because something wasn't right about him, and I was afraid of what he would have done.

When I left Jamaica, I was glad and thought I would never have to see him again, but I was dead wrong.

I should have told my mom what happened in Jamaica, but would it have changed anything? Would my mom have believed me? Who knows, all I know now is I'm a fool.

He let my face go and demanded, "Open your legs NOW!" in an aggressive but quiet voice. He said, "When I saw yuh in Jamaica mi fall in love."

I kept my legs closed shut and crossed my legs, restraining him from opening them. If I screamed, what would happen? *I should have dressed more like a boy around him and then this would not be happening,* I think to myself.

He applied pressure on my chest with his upper body and forced himself on top of me. He used his right hand to take his pants off slightly to remove his willy … his private part. Tears running down my face, I cried in silence and held my pants up while he tugged on them.

He pulled my pants down with force as I held on tight to pull them back up.

"Stop it, stop it, why are you doing this? I don't like it, stop!" I shrieked.

He slightly covers my mouth with his hand, "Shhhhhh…….yuh know yuh want it, yah nuh virgin suh open up NOW! Yah gwan like seh yuh nuh like mi," he says.

I cried and felt weak and went silent as he aggressively forced himself inside me with my legs still closed shut.

It felt big and hard, and he pushed harder. I questioned myself, "Is this how sex really feels?"

He squeezed my leg with his hand trying to weaken me to open but I wrapped my legs together tighter. He finally gave up as he got in at the tip, enough to give him a rise and release himself. He released himself on my leg. Then he got up and used his shirt to wipe my leg off and I lay there on my back motionless, wondering how I could be so stupid and not scream.

Why am I not screaming? What the hell is wrong with me? Open your mouth and scream! I speak to my inner self and still I remain lying there like a dumb dumb.

He got up and instructed me, "Pull up yuh pants" and questioned, "Yuh ah virgin?" with a pleased smile. I didn't respond and he threw the sheet on me and walked out quickly like a snake trying not to get caught while sneaking up.

I couldn't even find the strength to get up off the bed; I lay there like a dead body waiting for the autopsy.

"We live in fear and 'what ifs' instead of just living and speaking up. Release, speak and fuck the fear and what ifs. You are the person that has to live your life, not anyone else."

— Jenelle Simpson

CHAPTER 9

Instilled Fear

"Your next season is called, 'I'm winning regardless.' Your now season is preparation: 'I'm going to overcome any and all barriers that may try to get in my way.'"
Preparation Season = Winning Season.

– Jenelle Simpson

"I'm still learning to step outside of my comfort zone. Some days I push back when it feels uncomfortable, but discomfort taught me how to level up myself and not stand in stillness."

– Jenelle Simpson

I lay there and cried. I didn't know how long I'd been crying but I knew it was long enough, because it's now morning, Thursday morning, and of course I had to go to school, but just one more day to go.

I slowly got out of bed and looked in the mirror at my face. My eyes are bloodshot red and bulging from wasting my tears crying. I sluggishly walked over to my bedroom door and walked swiftly into the bathroom with my clothes in my hand.

God, what did I do wrong? How could I let this happen? This is all my fault. I should tell my mom! No, she won't believe me.

Mom, Uncle Tony, and my aunts all had told me that I should never let anyone touch me and if they do I should come and tell them, but why am I so afraid to go to them now and tell them what Uncle Ricky has been doing?

> "When you instill so much fear in a child and don't create a healthy environment where there is trust, openness, authentic communication and security, no matter how much you tell them they can tell you anything, fear will block them from coming to you about anything. Build a relationship with your children that is fearless, strong, brave, open, transparent, trusting, healthy and make them feel secure, so fear won't reside within them."
>
> – Jenelle Simpson

I closed the bathroom door behind me and locked it.

I turned on the water and let it run for approximately fifteen minutes just staring at it while it ran freely. I wished I was like water, flowing freely.

I climbed in the bathtub and sat inside while the water ran on my legs and the lower part of my body. The water feels good against my skin, soothing, and the rhythm of the water sounds like music to my ears. Water always calms me, along with music.

"DANIELLE, DANIELLE, DANIELLE, DANIELLE, DANIELLE!" Mom yelled.

I could hear her yelling my name, but I didn't respond.

I dried my tears instantly before I answered her so she didn't hear the shakiness in my voice.

Knock, knock, knock. Mom yelled, "Danielle, open the door!" while knocking at the door repeatedly".

I slowly got out of the shower. My vagina lips hurt and still felt slightly irritated, like a burning sensation. *How could I tell her?* I questioned myself again.

Mom wouldn't believe me. Even when Uncle Ricky and I are fighting, Mom ignores it and tells me to stop; she says I must have respect for my uncle. Respect for who? Someone who is hurting me? I could never respect him. Uncle Tony, on the other hand, always questions why we don't get along, as if he has some type of idea that something is going on, but he can't put his finger on it as of yet. Uncle Tony still does not like the thought of Uncle Ricky being here, so he always has his eyes on him.

When Uncle Ricky doesn't get his way and I argue with him, Mom would hear the arguments and he would lie and tell her I did something to him and that I am trying to provoke him. He even tells them that I hit him after he is the one who hits me.

I don't know if I should tell my mom what's been happening. Maybe she will notice something is wrong with me and I won't have to say much.

I dry my skin fast and open the bathroom door fast before she rips me open with her cussing this morning.

"Hurry up! You're going to be late for school. You didn't shower last night?" Mom yelled in a firm voice.

"Yes, Mom, I'm sorry, I wasn't feeling well, so I took a quick shower hoping that it would make me feel better," I responded.

"Are you sure you're okay?" Mom questioned with a concerned look on her face.

"Yeah, I'm okay," I responded.

I wasn't fine, but I told her I was, because I just didn't know how to tell her what I was going through. Talking to Mom is hard; she's stern and can be rough when she is ready.

I walked past mom and went into my room and closed the door. I slowly got dressed for school with tears rolling down my cheeks.

> **"We find it easier to hide the truth because lying convinces us that reality is not real. We lie to avoid telling the truth so we won't have to deal with the issue and the consequences and feel the pain, but the truth releases all the painful feelings. For me, a lie was easier than telling my mom what was happening, but it caused more damage. Don't let fear hold you back from releasing what needs to be released."**
>
> **- Jenelle Simpson**

Sarah left without me this morning and I was late for school. I could hear my mom yelling my name and cursing about me being late for school and something about how being late won't look good on my school record.

Mom takes education very seriously and hates when we are late unless she approves of it. I guess she's strict about school because she didn't get the full education she wanted. Mom has a hard time writing and reading sometimes, especially when it comes to pronouncing certain words. Mom usually has me write all her letters for her or I spell most of the words for her.

Mom always says, "Education is the key, take yuh book and nuh bodda waste nuh time."

I walked down the stairs as fast as I could, holding in my tears and holding onto a plastic smile so Mom didn't start questioning me. If I even mention Uncle Ricky's name she automatically thinks I'm just complaining and we're just fighting, nothing too serious for her to worry about.

"LALA, LALA come downstairs NOW!" Mom yelled. Lala is also my nickname, a nickname baby Krystal gave me.

I was already downstairs, but she didn't notice because she has been doing a million and one things in the kitchen.

I grabbed my backpack and lunch bag and rushed out the door quickly to avoid talking to her.

"Love you, see you later Mom!" I yelled.

"LALA, LALA!" I could hear her screaming my name and I knew it's because I didn't take my breakfast, but I'd be fine; I was not hungry.

It took me a while to get to school this morning. I wanted to vomit during my walk, but I took my mind into another dimension, thinking about when my mom, dad, brother, and I lived in our small apartment in Scarborough. I purposely walked slowly and dragged my feet because I didn't want to go to school.

I miss when it was only the four of us. We were happy and things were fine. Dad was so humble and just had his way of making Anthony and me happy. Our relationship with Dad isn't like my friends and their dads. Dad is so laid back and although I don't hear him say, "I love you" often, I know exactly how he feels about me. We are his "chargies," and we know he loves us deeply. Dad says we are his bonafide friends, not just his children.

Most of my friends spend time with their dads and talk to their dads about certain things or their dads are deadbeats. Although I had barely seen my dad since he and my mom had broken up, I don't think he is a deadbeat; he does what he can and what my mom allows him to. She calls him many names, but she restricts him from having the opportunity to see us and do more, so I say what she is saying is crap.

No one can come between the love and connection I have with my dad.

My mom cheated on my dad with Tony and my world changed. This is all her fault; if she had stayed with my dad, he would be here to protect me, but my mom had to destroy our lives. Dad is very serious about my brother and me. When something happens to one of us my dad would say, "Nuh mek mi head hurt mi yuh nuh, mi ah mod bloodclot mod mon…nuh ramp wid mi fucking pickney dem ehh ehhh."

I laugh out loud to myself, because Dad is crazy when he is mad, but it's so funny when he gets mad in his zone and starts stuttering.

When dad cusses it's so funny, we all laugh with him.

Mom hurt Dad, almost as if she got rich and just switched up on him when she met Tony. It was like she turned cold-hearted towards him.

I don't know if I will ever be able to forgive her for this, but dah well it's life; she does what she wants and when she wants. She was definitely attracted to Tony's lighter brown complexion, height, and big body.

"No one ever asks if the kids are okay with their decisions or pauses to think how it could possible affect the children. Pause, think and communicate with your children; it's essential to have deep-rooted conversations with them and consider their feelings before making big decisions that can possibly affect their lives."

- Jenelle Simpson

I finally arrived at school and went straight to the office for a late slip.

"Good morning," I said to the receptionist.

"Good morning, reason why you're late?" she replied.

I replied, "I woke up late."

I took the late slip and skipped the morning class, spending the morning in the bathroom, hiding, crying, and blaming myself for what happened. *I should start wearing baggier shirts and pants*, I whispered to myself.

I reason with myself, thinking of ways to make this stop, because I don't know if it's something I am doing to attract him to me.

I found a million reasons — things wrong with myself — for what happened last night. I officially labelled myself as a nasty coward.

"Ring, ring, ring!" The bell rings for lunch. I stayed in the bathroom the entire lunch break so I could pull myself together before anyone could notice something was wrong with me.

People came in and out of the bathroom and I could hear their conversations, them peeing and even taking number twos. I sat on the toilet seat and put my feet up to hide so no one could see that there was anyone in the bathroom stall.

I talked to myself and questioned myself, *Why, why me?* I whispered to myself quietly:

"God, what did I do wrong, did I do something to provoke him? Was I flirting with him? Did I unconsciously want him to do it and he knew?" I shake my head twice and mumble, "Ewww, he's my uncle, how could I have led him on? Shouldn't he know that I'm his niece and see me as such? We are family, why would he do this to me?"

I even contemplated running away, but where would I run to? I didn't have any money and I couldn't go to my family's house.

I spent the whole lunch break by myself, questioning why God would allow this to happen to me and why He wouldn't do something about it. Maybe I deserved it; maybe I had done something to someone in the past and this is my karma: pain, hurt, shame, and trauma.

Mom, Grandma Sweetie, and Dad always taught my brother and me that God will protect us, and we should never fear anything, but if that is true, then what is this? I don't see or feel any protection and I certainly don't hear him speaking to me.

> "When someone hurts us, especially someone that is close to us, we try to reason with our inner self and find excuses why the person did what they did. We try to see the good in them so, we start blaming ourselves and feel guilty that maybe we provoked the situation to happen. It is easier said than done, but be a constant reminder to yourself that someone else's pain inflicted on you is not your fault. Most people who inflict pain on others are going through their own silent war and you are just an outlet for them. There is purpose in the pain, trust God despite how it may look."
>
> – Jenelle Simpson

"TING! TING! TING!" It must be 12:45 p.m. which means the end of lunch, because the lunch bell is ringing.

I have to go to class now or else the teacher will mark me absent and Mom will kill me when I go home and question why I wasn't in class and Uncle Tony will beat me.

Uncle Tony beats us for everything. When I used to say my ABCs I used to say "'n" before the "Z," but really what I was saying was, "and Z," but Uncle Tony didn't like that, and he would beat me with his genuine leather slippers every time I did it. That slipper hurt and left welts on my legs. They beat first and ask questions later.

Mom allowed him to put his hands and objects on us, but I don't ever remember my own dad putting his hands on me. How could she allow a man who is not our biological father to beat us like that? It seemed as if he really enjoyed it, too.

I took my feet down from the toilet seat and got up, took a deep breath, opened the bathroom stall and left the bathroom. I started walking down the halls to go to class with my head down in shame.

I held my head down a lot as if I felt like people could see right through me and smell him on me.

> "When you've been violated or have some dark secret you feel like people can see right through you and sense that you are holding onto something."
>
> – Jenelle Simpson

"Hey! Where have you been? I've been looking for you! You okay?" Sarah questioned.

"DANIELLE, DANIELLE! HELLO!" Sarah yelled.

I responded with shock, "Yes, huh?"

I quickly turned, lifted my head and looked up. There she was with her wide marble nose staring at me as if she'd seen a ghost. Sarah grabbed my right arm, wrapped her left chubby arm around my arm linking them together like handcuffs, and we walked to class.

Sarah was talking but all I heard was "Blah blah blah blah." My mind was deep under the sea, and I was not interested in anything she had to say.

We were back in class sitting beside each other for the rest of the afternoon, but my mind and body were in another dimension as I replayed what had happened last night.

He touched me, he gripped me, and he forced himself on me and kissed me with his atrocious breath.

He's my uncle, is this normal, and why would he feel good doing this to me, his own niece? He even has a girlfriend and I'm a child.

I think to myself about how to get out of this disgusting mess. Should I tell Sarah? Maybe if I tell Sarah she will tell someone, but then …. no, never mind, I can't do that.

If I tell her she might look at me weird, or she may even judge me and not want to be my friend anymore, and I don't want to lose my friend. I don't want her to start stripping me down and treating me differently and think that "black" people are unpleasant.

> "It's hard opening up to people and telling them what we're going through, especially to the ones that we love. We don't know what to expect and we fear what their response will be. Start your breakthrough, let it out, and don't focus on the possibility of a negative response. How they choose to receive and respond has no burden on you."
>
> – Jenelle Simpson

CHAPTER 10

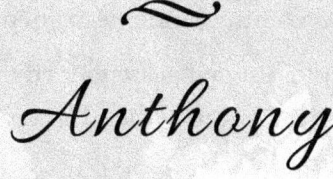

Anthony

I am Ready to Switch Things Up and Allow Myself to Learn and Receive New Things!

"We have to start switching things up and doing things differently. Just because you were raised that way doesn't mean you should continue the same toxic cycle and stay in the dark. Give yourself an opportunity to inhale and exhale new knowledge, breaking free from those generational cycles and creating new methods, ways, and experiences for yourself and future generations to come."

— Jenelle Simpson

3:30 p.m. It's home time and my heart was racing fast. I swear I felt a heart attack coming on. Did I even know what a heart attack felt like? No, but it sure did feel like my heart was about to explode or something. I had to go back home.

Today, I walked home without Sarah because I wanted to be alone and not talk to anyone.

My brother Anthony was coming home permanently today.

My mom decided he would just go back and forth from our house to school, so he could stay home with Krystal and me when Uncle Tony and she were at work.

Boy, was I excited to see him! I yelled, "I'm freeeee!" Now Uncle Ricky would never bother me again because my brother would be there to protect me, and I would stay with him everywhere he goes.

I walked home so fast it didn't take me too long to get there.

As I opened the front door, I heard loud voices and laughing coming from the basement, so I rushed downstairs and I saw my brother sitting beside Uncle Ricky talking about God knows what.

I nervously walked over to Anthony with an excited but painful smile on my face. I jumped on him, "Anthonyyyyyy!"

He smiled and brushed me off of him.

"What do you want, Elle," he grunted with a laugh in his voice.

I know he's just joking; he loves me. We have always been close and there for each other especially when we hear Uncle Tony and Mom fighting. Anthony always makes sure I'm good first ever since we were small. We are like twins and our bond is deep.

When Anthony is in a bad mood or hurt, I can feel it. I know when he is in his room listening to thought-provoking reggae music, he is writing music and in his zone. I hate to see him hurt or going through anything. I want to take all his painful emotions away.

I respond and question, "Nothing, just missed ya, what's up?"

"Miss you too, Lala, nothing…yuh good?" he responded with a smile and shook his head.

I turned my head and there he was with his jaundiced eyes staring at me and his big bottom lips looking disgusting and smooched up like a screw face.

He swore he was a *bod mon* and he was untouchable.

He mouthed something to me quickly.

"Go upstairs," he said.

Why was he talking to me and trying to tell me what to do? Big fool. I should tell my brother now what he has been doing to me, but a part of me feels guilty. My insides were still blaming myself and not wanting him to get in trouble, but I was not sure why I even felt this way.

I didn't want Anthony to look at me any differently than how he does now and worry about me. I am his baby sister.

I looked at Uncle Ricky with revulsion, wanting to scream to my brother and tell him what he did, but my lips are heavy; they felt numb, and I didn't know what to say. I became a mannequin for five whole minutes, but I still had a heartbeat. My ears were ringing, and my stomach started hurting. I slowly got up and walked upstairs, and my brother didn't even notice me slip away because his gums were still flapping; he was conversing with the bastard.

I walked up the stairs and headed to the second flight of stairs, slid straight into my bedroom, and put the blankets over my head.

"You're so stupid, why didn't you say anything? You caused this to come on yourself!" I whispered to myself as I cried and gasped for air.

My pillow was soaked, my head hurt, and I felt nauseous. I removed the sheets from my head and looked at my black alarm clock with red digital numbers showing 5:32 p.m.

I angrily get out of bed to go take a shower and do my homework before Uncle Tony gets home, so I won't get into trouble and get yelled at. Uncle Tony cursed and yelled about everything, especially when you don't do things on his schedule, such as bathing and finishing all of your homework.

I slammed the bathroom door, set a bath of warm water and sat inside the bathtub. I felt relaxed. I closed my eyes and let my head drop under the water.

I knew I shouldn't be getting my hair wet, but I didn't care; Mom could yell at me all she wanted to.

I thought about drowning myself, but that was too hard. I picked my head up, released the water from the tub, and turned on the shower head to wash off my body. I got out of the bathtub. I dried my chestnut brown skin with frustration and anger, whispering to myself, "If he comes to my room again, I will scream, everyone will hear me, and they will catch him in my room! Yeah, and he'll get thrown out of our house for good and things will go back to normal."

I rubbed every inch of my body with my raw shea butter, applied my entire face with Vaseline, and quickly put on my red cotton pajamas, pulling open the bathroom door and rushing out right into my room.

I rushed downstairs to eat my dinner, clean up the kitchen, and finish my religion homework as fast as I could before heading back to my bedroom.

I picked up my Bible and read Psalm 23:

> "The Lord is my shepherd; I shall not want.
>
> He maketh me to lie down in green pastures: he leadeth me beside the still waters.
>
> He restoreth my soul: he leadeth me in the paths of righteousness for his name's sake.
>
> Yea, though I walk through the valley of the shadow of death, I will fear no evil: for thou art with me; thy rod and thy staff they comfort me.
>
> Thou preparest a table before me in the presence of mine enemies: thou anointest my head with oil; my cup runneth over.
>
> Surely goodness and mercy shall follow me all the days of my life: and I will dwell in the house of the Lord for ever.
>
> Amen.
>
> (King James Version)

COMMITMENT TO A DECEITFUL LIAR

Mom said I should read this from my Bible every night before I go to bed and God will protect me.

As I begin to read, I question, *how is this supposed to protect me but I'm still afraid?*

I put my Bible on my night table still opened to Psalm 23 with tears rolling down my cheeks and started to pray.

> "God, thank you for waking me up this morning, protecting me and my family and making me have a safe day with my friends at school. Send your angels all around to protect me, my friends, teachers, homeless, needy, less fortunate, the workers, my grandparents, aunts, uncles, cousins, brother, sister and my parents. Dear God, give me the strength I need and protect me as I sleep. Amen."

I covered my head with my sheet and curled up like a ball, listening to see if there were any sounds coming towards my door.

I don't hear anything, so maybe he fell asleep.

I usually daydream before I go to sleep about the life I will have when I'm older, about my tall 6'1" minimum, caramel, baby-faced boyfriend who proposes to me and tells me how beautiful I am. The beautiful home we will have and our four gorgeous kids, three boys and one princess of the family. I dream about becoming a lawyer and looking professional and sexy in my cute outfits and suits. I dream about opening a big community center, a group center for youths, a place where youths can go any time and talk freely and get the help through life that they need. My husband is a businessman, a money-maker; I see him going through different stages in life, selling drugs but then becoming a successful businessman (not sure why I see him selling drugs). He is very caring, and we build an empire together. He has some rough edges, but he's soft when he needs to be and puts his family first. I trust him with our life; we pray together, travel, talk about every and anything, and most of all we trust and love each other unconditionally.

"Shut up yuh mouth, yuh chat too fucking much," I can hear Uncle Tony and Mom arguing. He is very bossy and demanding, and what he says goes, but Mom doesn't shut up when he says to shut up; she usually continues talking just to provoke him and show that she is a grown woman and no one can control her mouth.

Mom works the morning or afternoon shift, so she is home with us in the evening and/or the nights and Uncle Tony works the night shift 11:30 p.m. to 7:00 a.m. the next day.

They're home and that's my cue to go to sleep, my eyes slowly shutting down (snoring sounds).

CHAPTER 11

Penetration

"I tolerated so many things and kept quiet, because I didn't want to ruffle anyone's feathers, but while I was doing that, I caused internal damage to myself. Don't condone anyone's disrespectful behavior for fear of upsetting or losing them. Let them fly high. Accept only the best."

— Jenelle Simpson

"Creak creak creak creak creak," I heard the floors squeaking and my door opened lightly, waking me up. I am a very light sleeper and I hear everything in my sleep, and especially since Uncle Ricky has come to stay with us I haven't had a good night's rest. I can feel the light shining through my sheets. I was facing my wall, so I opened a tiny peephole and looked at my alarm clock; it's 1:02 a.m.

My legs were trembling. He was in my room, I can taste his smell on my tongue. I whispered to myself, "What do I do? Scream or stay quiet and maybe he will leave?"

He climbed into my bed and wrapped one of his rough-cut hands around my waist and put the other hand between my legs. Ricky does construction for work, so his hands are very choppy and rough.

I shut my legs and crossed them as tightly as I could. He tugged on my legs to open, but tonight I planned to fight and scream loudly enough for everyone to hear and catch him.

He put his hand around my neck and squeezed it, choking me from behind.

"Cough cough cough," I coughed, gasping for some release of air.

"Stop it, stop! I can't breathe, PLEASE!" I screamed in a soft and faint voice.

He responded in a stern voice. "Open your legs, yah guh mek me catch blue balls."

I think to myself, *What is blue balls, will it kill him?*

This is not how I planned it, I'm supposed to be screaming and fighting so that they would all hear and come into my room and catch him.

I questioned myself, "Why am I so afraid to scream, why is my body shutting down?"

He turned me over on my back with force, squeezed my face and said, "If you don't open your legs, I'll fuck you up."

I still kept my legs shut, and he held both of my legs on the inner thighs, pressing them with his nails piercing in my legs, and my legs begin to weaken, slowly opening like a cocoon. He took his right hand, pulled his pants down, removed his willy and forced it between my legs, enough to get past my vagina walls and partially into my temple.

I screamed, "OUCH! Please stop, I don't like it, it hurts, please, please, I won't tell anyone if you stop, please. I'm a virgin! Why are you doing this to me?"

He thrust his body up and down, in and out of me while groaning. The aggression gets harder, his willy gets harder, and it feels like it's growing and the pain progresses.

I softly cried, whispering to myself, "I want my mommy, I want my mommy."

He took both of his hands and forced both my legs open wider with anger that trembled my heart.

The in and out, up and down thrusting starts to get faster and he is panting with his breathing. He kissed my neck with his big rough dark pink lips.

He makes a big grunt "AHHHUGHH" and I can feel his willy gyrating … I think he is done. I feel something wet and warm running down my legs and on the front of my vagina as he gets off of me. I can smell it, too — it makes me feel nauseous.

What is it? I silently questioned myself.

I couldn't move; my hips, legs, and vagina are frozen and I feel as if I had lost all emotions in my body.

There was some gooey, slimy clear-white stuff coming out of me.

"OH MY GOD!" I yell softly, with tears coming down my face.

"I have to tell my mom, what am I going to do? This is gross, what is it?" I whisper to myself.

He looked at me with a pleased smile and whispered, "Shhhhhh, shut up before Claudette and Tony hear yuh."

He picked up my underwear and used it to wipe my legs with a rough scrub and whispered, in an obnoxious creepy voice, "Look at my sperm, it's rich yuh know how much baby dis."

He dropped my underwear on the bed by my left leg and said, "Go to the bathroom, clean up yourself and make sure yuh nuh tell nobody or else … no next mon fi touch yuh….yuh hear."

His accent was so strong and rough, but I knew what he meant: no other man other than himself is allowed to touch my body and have me the way he does. I questioned myself, *What would he do if I told someone, is he a serial killer or something?*

I lay there and watched him leave the room like the thief in the night that he is.

I cried and cried and didn't get up because the pain was so unbearable, the way he penetrated and jerked my body made me feel like the chickens Grandma used to slaughter in Jamaica.

I got up slugging over looking at my alarm clock. It's 2:25 a.m., and I was holding the bottom of my stomach and dragging my feet as I walked to the bathroom silently, making sure no one could hear me.

I slowly slipped into the bathroom just in case Uncle Tony had fallen asleep on the couch, as he does most nights, in his boxers watching TV. I could hear him snoring so loudly, but their room door is closed so I knew they were both in there sleeping and all the lights were off in the house. Mom has nightlights plugged in all over the house, because she believes when it's too dark duppies (ghosts) will come.

I gently closed the bathroom door and turned on the tap water, grabbed my rag, put soap on it and started scrubbing my skin. I used the rag to wipe my vagina and leg off. I wanted to just jump in the shower and scrub his nasty smell and impression from my body, but if I turned on the shower Mom and Uncle Tony would hear the loud water sounds and wake up. They would hear me, and I would get in big trouble. I didn't want Uncle Tony yelling at me, so I continued scrubbing my skin so hard I accidentally cut myself on my right forearm with my fingernail … just a little scratch with a bit of blood, nothing to freak out about!

I ended up wetting up the bathroom mat on the floor by the sink with some water. I quickly picked up the mat and tried to squeeze out some of the water. I rested it on the top of the bathtub hoping that it would be dried by morning and Mom wouldn't notice. Mom notices everything and she complains and curses about every small thing, as well.

Her yelling is scarier than getting beatings from Uncle Tony.

I wetted the rag with lukewarm water a second time and applied it to my vagina area to soothe the irritated feeling, and then put the rag in the bathtub.

I put on a new pair of underwear, a T-shirt, and a pair of pants. I stared at myself in the mirror for a few minutes and looked at myself in disgust, wondering why would I let something like that to happen to me again. *How dumb can I be?* Uncle Tony doesn't even like him, so if I screamed, I knew Uncle Tony would have woken up and killed him. I keep staring at myself thinking about hurting myself but I couldn't. I turned off the bathroom lights, opened the door, and went back into my bedroom.

I closed my bedroom door completely, and my fear of the dark suddenly went away, and I now had a new fear. I sat on the edge of my bed, took a deep breath, exhaled, and burst out bawling. I wanted to scream out loud, but I couldn't, so I screamed on the inside and began to speak to God:

"God, what did I do wrong? Is it because I don't pray to you when my mom tells me to and you're now punishing me for not listening to her? Please tell me, what did I do, please?"

Mom taught me that whenever I am going through something, anyone is bothering me, or I am afraid, I must call on Father God and that's what I am doing, but I can't hear him. "Where are you God when I need you?"

Mom told me God protects us from the enemy and harm, so where is God to protect me from me? WHERE?

I sat on my bed questioning God and crying till my chest hurt; it felt as though I was gasping for air, but the air is all gone and I am choking. Have you ever cried to the point you can't breathe, and you wish you weren't alive? Well, that's me right now and the feeling is strong.

I got up, picked up my underwear which he had used to wipe my leg off, and wrapped it into a small ball. I take one of the small garbage bags Mom had given to me from my closet. I had these small garbage bags in my room to throw my pads in there discreetly, so no one knows when I am on my period or sees my pads in the bathroom garbage. Mom said I am a young lady, and I should be clean and respectable when it comes to my period.

My mom didn't teach me much about my period — it was Aunty Korraine who had talked with me. I had my first period at Aunty Korraine's house, and she was so excited to help me and talk to me about it, something Mom didn't do. Aunty Korraine explained that now that I have my period I should be very careful with boys, not to let them touch me, and now I can get pregnant.

I put the bag in the front of my school bag in the small front pocket so I can throw it away tomorrow on my way to school, so Mom won't see it and start questioning what had happened to me.

I am so afraid to tell my mom and I still don't know how, but I know the outcome won't be in my favor.

I took my school bag and put it back into my closet, closed the door, and climbed into bed. As I pulled my sheet to cover my body, I could smell his odor still on my sheets. I could see his face in my bed, and I felt nauseous wondering if he would come back for me again for more. I lay my head on my wet pillow – it was soaked with my tears, and I closed my eyes and cried myself to sleep.

> "The way we plan things don't always turn out the way we planned. Sometimes we expect roses and pearls, but God has his own plans for our lives, good or bad it's always purposeful."
>
> – Jenelle Simpson

CHAPTER 12

Personality Shift

"Some days you may feel like a mess and attacked, but God has placed a protective cloak inside and outside you. <u>YOU ARE SEALED UP AND PROTECTED</u>."

— Jenelle Simpson

"Danielle, Danielle, Danielle, wake up it's time to get ready for school. Why does your room smell funky?" Mom questioned.

I kept my head covered with my sheets with my eyes closed, trying to pull myself together before I faced Mom.

"Okay, Mom, I am getting up now, sorry and I don't know," I replied.

Mom opened my bedroom windows so fresh air could air out my room and she left to head downstairs to probably get my breakfast ready.

I slowly got out of bed, dreading having to do anything today. I could smell his disgusting body odor and cologne left behind.

I took my school clothes and underwear out of my drawer, grabbed my towel, went to the bathroom, and locked the door behind me.

I got into the shower and turned on the shower head to take a quick shower so Mom doesn't even notice. I used mostly hot water to scale off all his residue left on me. I scrubbed my skin with my melon and strawberry soap. I scrubbed and I scrubbed in hopes that I would scrub him off of me and wash away the feeling I was having.

I could hear Mom screaming my name, "Danielle, Danielle, come downstairs for your breakfast and hurry up and go to school."

I wished I could block her out and I didn't have to listen to her. I don't know when I started hating her, but I do, and I wished she wasn't my mother at times, but yet I love her to death. She should have never left my dad for this pig TONY! She shouldn't have allowed her brother to move in with us.

I turned off the water and watched it flow down the drain slowly. My naked body stands in the tub, and I am scared to get out, but I slowly held onto the bathtub and climbed out. I grabbed my white towel and dried my body slowly and delicately. My vagina lips were still burning a bit and my legs were wobbly, but I stood strong, moisturized my skin with my shea butter, and got dressed in a rush before Mom could come upstairs and see me not dressed for school. I gently used my face scrub and face cloth to wash my face and then I brushed my teeth.

I opened the bathroom door gently, peeped out the door to make sure he wasn't standing there waiting, turned off the bathroom lights, and walked into my bedroom. I shut the door behind me as softly and gently as I could. His bedroom door was open wide, but I didn't think he was in there because the lights were off. He must have left for work already. "Dirty bastard," I whispered to myself.

I opened my closet door, picked up my backpack and strolled down the stairs. My walk was a bit different this morning but I tried to walk normally so Mom didn't notice anything different with me. I walked into the kitchen.

"Good morning, Uncle Tony," I said.

"Good morning, why you wake up suh late?" Uncle Tony questioned.

"I wasn't feeling well and I overslept, sorry," I replied.

I responded quickly because I knew that stare he was giving me and I didn't want him to start yelling.

"Okay, hurry up and go to school," he replied.

I picked up my baby sister Krystal who was sitting in her highchair drinking her cornmeal porridge from her baba. I started kissing her on her chubby soft cheeks and she stared at me with her big bright eyes, spooling out love at me. I felt my eyes overflowing with tears. Her facial expression changed as she looked at me; she can sense I am not happy and suddenly she started to cry as if someone had pinched her and Mom jumped.

"Danielle, what did you do?" Mom said.

"Mom, I didn't do anything, she's just mad because her baba came out of her mouth, she's so greedy," I replied.

"I'm not hungry, I have to leave. I'm going to be late for school," I added with my head held down.

"You need to eat, here's a piece of toast with jam," she said as she passed me the toast wrapped up in white paper towel along with a juice box.

I took the piece of toast, the juice box, and my lunch bag from her. I walked away to the door, put on my school shoes, and opened the door to leave.

"Bye Krystal, Uncle Tony, and Mom," I said.

"Okay, have a good day at school," Mom replied.

Mom rushed out of the kitchen to catch me before I closed the door, placed her hand on my head and began to pray:

> "God please cover her under your blood and keep her safe, no harm shall come her way. Amen."

Mom kissed me on my head, and I rushed out of the house but then walked very slowly to school.

"Heyyyyyyyyyyy girl, DANIELLLLLLEEEEEE!"

I heard someone yelling out my name, and I turned around and I saw Sarah running behind me, wobbling and screaming as if she was an insane woman.

Sarah stopped running and said, "Why did you leave so early? I just rang on your door and your mom said you just left. You okay?" Sarah questioned.

I looked at Sarah and replied, "Yes! I wasn't sure if you were coming this morning, because you didn't call me back last night."

Sarah replied, "You know I come to your house every morning. Are you sure you're okay? You don't look okay. Were your parents arguing again this morning?" Sarah questioned.

I responded in an aggravated voice, "No, I'm sure! I'm okay and Tony is not my father, so stop calling him that … I hate when you call him my parent, my father, stepfather, or my mom's husband … BECAUSE HE'S NONE OF THESE THINGS!"

Sarah looked at me a little fearfully and as if I was weird, but I was not crazy… I was perfectly fine… I just, I just, ughhhh, I didn't even know anymore what I was.

Sarah reached out for me with both her arms open, waiting for me to accept her enormous bear hug, but I stood still with not even a blink of an eye, so she walked closer to me with her arms still open.

"Come here my little baby, it's otay I love you," she said in her squeaky chipmunk voice, and she gave me one of her special bear hugs that feels so warm and safe.

Sarah did not deserve me yelling at her, but I was just frustrated. She didn't even get mad at me for the tone I just hit her with — honestly I'm not sure what I would do without her friendship. She's such an amazing friend and I wish I could just dump it all on her and let her in, but no!

We continued our walk to school as Sarah yaps and yaps about how cute and sexy Kevin is. I didn't say much; I just listened to her, smiled, shook my head in agreement, and walked as if I were a zombie.

We finally arrived at school and the day went by fast. I stayed inside for the entire recess, pretending to catch up on homework and claiming that I wasn't feeling well. I mean I was not feeling well, but not ill. Sarah kept trying to cheer me up, but I ignored her every time she spoke to me and kept asking me what was wrong. I felt like yelling at her again to get off my back, but all she was doing was trying to help me to cheer up.

> "Good friends that go the extra mile to check in and cheer you up are worth more than money itself. Appreciate the ones that understand you even in silence."
>
> – Jenelle Simpson

It was the end of the day and the teacher was explaining our "big" project assignment to us, something about researching our music idol and "blah blah blah blaze blaze" BORINGGGG!!!

I already knew who I was going to do my research on, "MARIAH CAREY!" I yelled out loud by accident.

"What did you say, Danielle?" Mr. Roberts asked me.

"Nothing, sorry Sir," I responded quietly. Embarrassed, I shrank in my seat.

"TING, TING, TING, TING, TING!" … the dismissal bell was going off.

I grabbed my backpack quickly, started putting my books into my bag, and got ready to leave while the teacher was still rambling on.

"You guys brainstorm over the weekend and start your research and have a great weekend," Mr. Roberts said to us.

I quickly and smoothly drifted out of the classroom door before anyone noticed me and hovered all over me to walk home with me.

I rushed out the school doors, not in a rush to get home, but in a rush to get away from everyone. School is my escape, but as days go by, I just feel naked, as if they could see right through me and were stripping me down mentally. I felt like they could see that I was hiding something and as if they were judging me.

I took the long way home and walked very slowly while talking and singing to myself. Although I'm not a "singer," I love singing and it gives me comfort, especially when I'm feeling sad.

My mom and Uncle Tony were both working the afternoon shift today, so they wouldn't be home until after midnight, so it's just Anthony, baby Krystal, that PIG, and me.

Unfortunately, Krystal had turned one year old on February 18th, several weeks ago, so Mom's maternity leave was finally up, and she had to jiggy back to work. Mom is a registered nurse and she works at two different hospitals right now; both were in downtown Toronto, but I was not sure where she was working tonight. Uncle Tony is also a registered nurse, which I thought was a weird choice for a male to work. He works at a nursing home and also at a hospital in downtown Toronto.

"Ugghhhhhhhh," I faintly grunted under my breath.

I mean, of course, I love Krystal and I had always wanted a baby sister; I always wanted a lot of siblings so I wouldn't need friends. Often I feel like she's my responsibility, like my child to take care of when Mom is not around.

And I wished she'd come about with a better choice of "stepdad." He's not what I imagined my stepdad would be. I pictured someone nicer, someone friendlier, approachable, odorless, and more like-minded like my real dad.

COMMITMENT TO A DECEITFUL LIAR

"ACTUALLY, WAIT! I NEVER WANTED A DAMN STEPDAD. I WANT MY REAL DAD BACK AND MY MOM UGHH," I yelled to myself, screaming on the inside with a high-pitched voice.

"I am crazy aren't I, yup!" I opened my mouth and wished to myself softly that Uncle Tony wasn't in our lives and that mom and dad would get back together.

Dah well, it is what it is and he's here and he is the "MAN OF THE FUCKING HOUSE…" in his words daily.

I laugh in my head — I felt like I was going mad, talking to myself more often.

I turned quickly on Mulberry Street to head over to the convenience store to get some treats for my sister, brother, and myself.

I ran through the alley and rushed into the store, right over to the big blow pops—my favorite. I picked up a few, the extra one for me, along with some small key rings. I hand the cashier an change.

"Thank you," the cashier said.

"You're welcome," I responded.

I walked out of the store slowly because it hit me again, and my stomach starts to cringe as I realize that I have to go home.

"Lord, please don't let him be home yet, God, please," I grunted out loud to myself as I dragged myself to walk home.

I started singing and dancing on my way home, this time "Ting-A-Ling" by Shabba Ranks.

I was singing in my sweet island girl voice, reminiscing about my young days back home in Jamaica. I don't remember too much, but I remember slightly a bit.

Wooiiiiiiiiiii, I love this song from when I was a little girl. This has always been one of my favorite songs.

"Booyaka! Booyaka! – I yelled out as a skanked my foot in a dancing motion as I walked.

That is a little piece of my favorite part of the song.

I saw Uncle Tony about to get into the car to leave for work, but he spotted me and stopped. Uncle Tony was also on the evening shift today, so when he and Mom were done with work, he would pick her up and they would drive together.

Kiss my teeth… he's just staring at me like he has no sense.

"Waum gyaly," Uncle Tony said.

"Gyaly," my dad gave me that nickname, and who gave Mr. Tony the permission to start using it? He is really trying to be my dad and impersonating everything he does. What a rip off!

"Hi, Uncle Tony, see you later," I responded.

"Alright, lata. Mek sure yuh do yuh homework and bathe. Mom left dinner for you guys and food for Krystal," Uncle Tony said.

"Okay, bye," I replied.

I walked past the garage, around the corner and stepped up the stairs. The door was still open, so I didn't have to use my keys. I slowly pushed the door open and closed it behind me. I slowly took off my shoes like a ghost in the night, slid open the closet door with Krystal's sticky fingerprints on the mirror attached to it, put down my shoes, and closed the door swiftly.

I saw Uncle Ricky's work shoes, so I know he's home, but I don't hear Anthony, so I guess he's not home yet from school, and again I am stuck with baby Krystal and this Jamaican runt.

I picked up my knapsack, threw it over my shoulder, tiptoed around the corner, and headed up the stairs, clenching my body muscles so I didn't make a sound that would give away my presence.

I stopped at the second level of the stairs — there she is, my fatty boom boom sleeping soundly in her playpen, peaceful with no worry or pain on her shoulders.

"God, I pray she never experiences pain," I whispered out loud to myself, but quietly enough that no one could hear me.

I reached into her playpen and pet her hair like she's my little puppy and walked away straight into my room. I shut the door behind me and do a big release.

"SIGH!" I breathed out and released it.

I put my knapsack in my closet, closed the door and stared at my bed in disgust. I wished I could burn the bed and burn him in it. Just grab a match, tie him to the bed and throw the match on while he screams and begs for mercy.

I lay on my bed in hopes to take a nap since Krystal was sleeping and I didn't need to attend to her right now. I could definitely take a quick nap before she would wake up.

I loved babysitting Krystal, and of course I didn't mind doing things for her to help Mom, but sometimes I felt stiffened to have to take care of her as if she was my child, and I felt like my own childhood freedom was being taken away from me. Mom called me to do everything for her. I wondered what it would be like when I am older, a teenager. Would she become my full-time responsibility, would I be caring more for her like she is my daughter and babysitting her and dragging her around behind me?

Welp! I guess I really didn't have a choice, so I just had to deal with it until I was able to leave and live on my own.

"Your children are not your children's children, stop transferring parenthood responsibilities onto your children. Allow your children to grow and enjoy childhood without taking on the role and burden of becoming parents at a young age."

— Jenelle Simpson

CHAPTER 13

Paradise

"I woke up many mornings feeling like a train wreck, a flood of memories from the past tried to drown and re-traumatize me. I felt so down and upset, but then I stood up and repeated: 'I am more than a conqueror, I defeated that, and I am present.'

Don't let that feeling ruin your day and where you are now; shake it off."

— Jenelle Simpson

COMMITMENT TO A DECEITFUL LIAR

I fell asleep pretty quickly. I was so tired because I had spent most of the night being on lookout as if I was a neighborhood watchdog. It has become such a routine for me to stay up, praying and hoping that he didn't come to visit me. He was such a creep. How could this man really be my uncle, this man cannot be my uncle … maybe he is adopted and just a sick bastard.

This nap feels so good and for once I actually feel safe sleeping even if it's just for a moment. My dreams are always so comforting and refreshing to remember the beauty of Jamaica. I really miss being there and taking in the fresh, fresh breeze.

"Grandma Sweetie, I missed you so much!" I said, and I jumped up and hugged her.

"Move from yah suh, ahhhhhhh God yuh get big eee mon," Grandma Sweetie responded.

Grandma couldn't believe how big I had gotten; she created such an excitement as she stared at me and hugged me.

"Kim, Kim, Kim!" Sweetie yells out to Aunty Kim.

"Yes, mama! Mi ah come!" Kim responded.

I see the curtain that covers the front doorway open up and there she is, Aunty Kim. She looks at me with surprise, runs over to me, and hugs me up so tight. Her hug makes me feel so welcome, wanted — a hug I've been longing for. Someone to hold me tight and tell me everything is going to be all right.

My dream feels so real, it actually feels like I'm being hugged in the present and her arms are wrapped around me as I sleep, sheltering me and rocking all my pains away. I wish my dream was a reality and I could tell my aunty all that was happening, and she would protect me, take me away, and hide me.

"Yuh know how long yuh leff yah, yuh get so big and still pretty," Kim says. Aunty Kim thinks I grew so sweet and pretty, but little did she know I was so insecure and didn't really see the beauty she saw in me. Even so, her compliment made me feel so confident and gave me a self-boost.

> "Sometimes we may not feel so great about ourselves, and a small compliment can make us feel so amazing about ourselves and strike a spark within us. A person can make you begin the first stages of self-love, deep connection with self and that is something great."
>
> – Jenelle Simpson

I smile, pleased with her compliments because although I'm so young, I am extremely insecure about the way I look. My mom still made me wear bubbles up until recently. I don't look nothing named grown!

"Thank you, Aunty, how are you?" I respond.

"Come inside nuh muss tiyad, plane ride long eee," Kim says.

Wow! The inside looks the same as when I left, nothing has really changed: the rooms, the beds, and that porch. Although I don't really remember what the place looks like since I left at such a tender age, I can feel the atmosphere and it feels the same. I love it here.

"Danielle, yuh nuh have boyfriend, right?" Aunty Kim questions.

I giggle, "No! I'm too young," I respond, a little surprised that she would think someone like me would have a boyfriend. She is absolutely cray cray.

"Danielle, Danielle, Danielle, where are you?" I heard Anthony yelling my name.

I could hear Anthony screaming my name as I jumped up out of my sleep quickly and am shocked, why he was screaming my name so loudly?

Although he scared the heck out of me as I came out of my sleep, boy, I'm so glad that he is home from school.

Anthony has to take a few buses to get home, so we don't get home at the same time. Most of the time he gets home before me, but other times he doesn't come straight home from school.

I jumped up out of bed, swung my bedroom door open, and with suspense squirmed into my brother's room, which is right next door to mine. His back is turned facing the door.

I squeezed him from behind and bit him on his arm.

"Big Batty Tickle!" I yelled out. "Big Batty Tickle" is the nickname my brother had from he was younger and we were living in Jamaica, because he has a round, high big butt like basketball player buttocks behind him.

He doesn't seem to like the name, but it grew on him, and he's used to it now, so too bad.

"Ouch yuh brute, why did you bite me for?" he responded as he laughed with his contagious laugh just like my dad. My brother and I both laugh and smile the same as our dad and it gives me great pleasure having a brother that reminds me of my dad. As the old Jamaican saying goes, "my dad cut him right out ah nuh jacket or vest.....hahaha," I laughed in my head.

Not having my dad around anymore has been hard for me to adjust to, but my brother has been filling his shoes and is a huge asset in my life. Anthony is really like my father; he cares for me just the same as a father would and never makes me feel left out.

We are really close; we are like BFFs, I mean not really, but yeah, we are close like besties.

He tells me everything, even about his girlfriends, and I tell him some things. Sometimes I try to nosy myself in his business and he will cuss me out, but meh, doesn't bother me.

"Mom left dinner for us in the oven and left us a note that she will call us on her break at work."

"RING, RING, RING, RING, RING, RING, RING, RING!" The phone is ringing, that must be Mom now calling to check up on us.

"Hello," I said as I picked up the phone.

"Hi Lala, how are you? How was school?" Mom asked.

"I'm good and school was okay," I responded.

"Where's your brother?" Mom questioned.

"He's right here," I responded.

"Mek mi talk to him" Mom said.

"Hey, what's up mama," Anthony said to Mom.

"Just here on my break, eating some dinner. How was school?" Mom responded.

"It was good still. Mom, I need some money please," Anthony said.

"Weh yuh need money fah now?" Mom responded.

"Lunch money, wah yuh mean?" Anthony responded with his contagious giggle.

"Yuh always want money, money," Mom responded.

"Alright, bye Mom, see you tomorrow," Anthony said.

"Okay, let me speak back to yuh sista deh son," Mom responded.

"Yes, Mom," I took the phone from Anthony's hand, a little annoyed because sometimes she just loves to talk and ramble on about absolutelyyyyyyyyyy nothing! I screamed in my head.

"Yuh sure yuh alright?" Mom questioned with a whispering voice.

"Yes, I am!" I respond.

"Okay, I'll come see you when I come home and don't forget to rub the thing behind your ears and on your forehead before you go to bed. Rub some pon yuh bredda too please," Mom instructed.

"Okay Mom, bye," I responded.

My mom gave me this tiny, clear bottle with some brown liquid stuff on the inside, just like the one she rubs on us in the morning, and it smells strong, like an old woman's fragrance. "Barf." I mean it smelled bad and I don't understand why she says we must rub it behind our ears before bed and wear it to school. I mean some days I pretend like I'm using it, or she'll rub it on me herself, but Anthony and she always fight about it. He hates when she tells him to use it and he never does.

Anthony would get mad and cuss her out, and then she would tell me to sneak and rub some behind his ears. I knew it was wrong, so sometimes I would lie to her and tell her I did it, but I really hadn't.

Anthony thinks Mom is dumb when she says some stuff and doesn't believe or buy into things that she says.

Mom claims it's to protect us and keep us safe, but only God can keep us safe and that's the belief I stand by. I'm not sure how some oil can keep us safe and ward off bad energy; this lady is crazy for real.

Anthony calls it obeah oil and he says *move that shit away from me* all the time.

"Some people believe in other powers, different gods that they worship and material things, but there's only one God that many have different names for. The highest form of power comes directly from God. God is above and is all things."

— Jenelle Simpson

I walked away to head over to my room.

"Anthony, I'm going to go shower before you and then go eat," I said.

"Okay, hurry and don't take long you brute," Anthony responded.

I slowly paced into my room and closed the door. I opened my drawer beside my bed that had all my underwear. I pulled out a pair of purple underwear with some squiggly designs on them. Then I headed over to the other side of the room where my clothes were in my drawer and pulled out my nightgown.

My door opened slowly, and I could feel a presence peeping in. I turned my head and there he was walking into my room ... for what reason?

"What's up, I missed you today and mi buddy stiff," Ricky said, staring at me with his jaundiced eyes and his nasty morning breath although it's not even morning.

He took a closer step towards me, bringing his hand close to me, and put his hand on my stomach before roughly shoving his hand down my pants. His hand reaches the top of my vagina, and I can feel his rough, bruised working hands chipping away at me. He tries to move in a circular motion, and I grab his hand as hard as I could with my nails piercing into his hands, but he clinches back.

"Yo mi ah guh wan some of diss tonight and memba if yuh tell nuh body mi will lick off yuh face," Ricky added, and looked at me with death in his eyes.

I stared at him silently with tears filling my tear ducts, grinding my teeth, but no tears come out.

I stood strong and held my tears back because I wanted to appear strong, not scared and let him know that I was not going to back down and I was not afraid of him, despite the fact that I was terrified.

"Get out," I said to him.

He turned away and left my room. I could hear him turn the corner to head over to my brother's room.

I remember one morning he kept trying to get to me and I didn't know what to do, so I called Sarah and asked her to come to my house early. It was him and I home alone. I purposely did everything so he couldn't get to me—I called my mom at work, and I stayed on the phone. I locked the bathroom door and he tried to break it open.

He had even started hitting me, punched me in my face and choked me; I tried my best to put up one hell of a fight the best way I knew how.

When Sarah came to the house and I was leaving with her, he started cussing at me, calling me a bitch and telling me I don't know who I am ramping with, threatening me that he would murder me, "bloodclot." While I was walking with

Sarah, he picked up one of the big bricks from Mom's little dead side garden and threw it at me, nearly taking off my entire head.

Sarah was terrified and asked what the heck that was, but I ignored her as if it were nothing.

He had beaten me so badly my body was in pain for days, but I knew how to play it off as if I was perfectly fine in front of everyone, as I knew when he said he would fuck me up, he would.

CHAPTER 14

~

Blame It On Voodoo

Release and Refresh

"Don't put boundaries on your manifestation. Believe in your ability to create and succeed in what you are manifesting."

– Jenelle Simpson

COMMITMENT TO A DECEITFUL LIAR

I remember back when Uncle Ricky first came to live with us, there was a big excitement about him not being normal or himself. They claimed that he was sick and his best friend worked voodoo on him to stop him from coming to Canada, because he was jealous of him, and his friend was trying to hold him down in life (keep him at the bottom of life), so Grandma had to go to Jamaica and get him cleaned up (cured). I don't know why she had to travel all the way back to Jamaica for this "cure," but Dad had taught me that only God can heal men and women and that I must not listen to all that obeah stupidness, as he calls it.

Sweetie brought back a bottle of brown medicine for him to drink daily and some other products that he had to take and bathe in.

They blame his behavior on the obeah and claimed he was not right (conscious) in his mind and that his friend was trying to mod him. I think he is 1,000,000% conscious and knows what he is doing and there's nothing wrong with him.

Everything that goes wrong or looks wrong they give power to obeah. Having a mental breakdown, "ah some body obeah yuh, yuh betta guh get wash off and clen up yuhself."

Having any type of problem in life, ah obeah.

> "When people have a hard time accepting the truth and things for what it really is, they try to find reasons and things to blame for what is happening. Learn to accept things for what they really are, inhale and exhale and deal with it, stop searching for excuses and playing the blame game."
>
> – Jenelle Simpson

"Wah gwan Anthony, everything good?" Ricky asked.

"Yeah yeah, everything bless," Anthony responded.

"Mi ah beg yuh warn yuh sista yuh nuh, because mi nuh wan do har nun," Ricky said.

"What did she do?" Anthony questioned.

"She always a violate me and a try fuck round me," Ricky responded.

"Okay, I will talk to her," Anthony responded while laughing.

"Yah come downstairs to eat?" Ricky questioned Anthony.

"Yeah, just now just doing something first … soon come," Anthony responded to Ricky.

I headed into the bathroom to bathe, terrified of what's going to happen tonight. I just didn't know what I should do because if I say anything they may not believe me, and I needed proof. Mom and the entire family might hate me and think I am a liar.

I slowly took off my clothes and jumped into the shower. I turned on the pipe so quickly and hard that I almost broke the handle out of anger.

My body wash was done so I used the Dove bar soap to lather my rag, rub all over my body, and then I threw water all over my skin to rinse off the soap and turned off the pipe. I'm done — less than five minutes it took me to shower today because I just wanted to go to my bed and be away from that maggot.

I dried my skin, put on my clothes, and threw my towel on the hook behind the washroom door.

I came out of the bathroom and headed downstairs to eat my dinner; my brother had shared out my portion and left it on the table for me already.

"Thank you," I said to Anthony.

"You're welcome Pootus," Anthony responded. (Pootus is also one of my nicknames.)

I pulled out the chair at the end of the table with my head down and sat in front of my food. I stared at the food first for a quick minute before I even started to eat …white rice, cabbage, and bully beef (corned beef)!

I picked up my fork and started playing with the rice.

My appetite went away; my stomach instantly became full when I sat down, and I'm turned off.

"Suh yuh nah guh eat," Anthony said.

"Yeah, I'm just not hungry anymore … maybe because I waited too long to eat," I responded.

"Eat your food and shut up. Well mi ah guh eat because ah hungry mon is an angry man," Anthony responded.

"Suh Anthony, yuh nah gimme one ah yuh gyal dem," Ricky said.

"Which gyal yah talk bout dog," Anthony responded.

"Mi know seh yuh have nuff gyal ah hide, gimme one mek mi fuck and stop move like a big pussy," Ricky responded.

"Ahhhh hahaha, you're a funny guy," Anthony said, smiling and laughing. "Dog yuh funny, alright mi will line up a ting."

"Mi ah come home early from work tomorrow," Ricky said, "Claudette ah guh ah work and yuh step fadda? We cyaan invite two gyal ova and ting."

"I don't know, but we will see tomorrow," Anthony said.

Ricky said it as if he was trying to get a rise out of me and trying to stir up some emotions in me that will never ever be there even if he dropped dead.

Anthony and Uncle Ricky had their differences as well, Uncle Ricky talks way too much, thinks he knows it all and can be very disrespectful to everyone and anyone except Uncle Tony.

One time Uncle Ricky must have said something rude to Anthony about his "white" girlfriend and they started physically fighting. Mom was screaming down the place telling them to stop, but Uncle Ricky thinks that he can just do what he wants whenever and however.

He looked up at me with a smile on his face, his eyes speaking to me as if he's waiting to get a reaction out of me, so he can start a fight with me. His eyes spoke to me and pulled me from the inside, telling me he wanted me to be upset that he is asking about a girl. He talked about girls very often around me as if he was trying to get me jealous and annoyed, but he does not realize I didn't care.

He poked his fork into the rice and the bully beef, scooped it up, put the fork in his mouth, and started to take bites. His mouth moves so fast and ekkk, he has no table etiquette.

I can feel his nasty burnt-looking dark red lips still on my skin. It's like a permanent mark.

"Don't look at me," I blurted out.

"Ah who ah look pon yuh, fuck off," Ricky responded.

I don't say anything in response because Anthony is over-protective of me and I don't want them to be fighting because of me. He doesn't like conflict, and this is going to be one.

He pulled me out and I've been sitting here trying not to let him get under my skin ughh!

Ricky and I always fought and we just did not get along, but no one cared enough to figure out why a child would hate their own uncle so much. No one could hear or see my silent cries.

I finally started eating my food with my head down and facing the plate. The entire time my eyes were fixed on my plate.

All I could taste is bitterness in my mouth. I didn't even know what the food tasted like anymore. All I knew was, it was done and it was time for me to go upstairs and get ready for bed.

I lifted my hands slowly, placed my palms on the edge of the table, and pushed my chair aggressively but very slowly against the floor, so it doesn't scrape my mom's precious tiled floors. Mom is always complaining "mind yuh scratch up mi floor, cuz mi work hard fi dis," – I replayed Mom's annoying voice in my head.

I slowly stood up and picked up my plate. I walked over to the garbage by the sink, emptying what was left on my plate into the garbage, and put my plate in the sink.

I started putting all of the containers with the food back in the fridge, when I saw him walking towards me from the side of my eye. Look at his scrawny legs in those ugly light brown shorts and his white shirt … he looks so disgusting, and I just can't stand the sight of him, his smell, his walk, and his stance beside me make me want to scream so loud and punch him.

He placed his plate on the counter, looked at me and grinned with that big gap in between his top teeth.

"Empty dat and wash dat," Ricky said to me, with an entitled, powerful, but soft voice.

"Hmmm," Anthony said, with a disappointed look on his face.

Anthony knew Ricky and I didn't get along at all, but he never seemed to care why because he has never asked why or bothered to say anything.

Ricky walked off and started walking up the stairs.

"Goodnight children, see you tomorrow," Ricky turned around and said to Anthony and me.

I did not respond.

"Alright, lata," Anthony responded.

I started washing the dishes and cleaning up the kitchen.

"I'm going to bathe, you okay Danielle?" Anthony said.

"Yes, I'm okay, just going to finish cleaning up and then head up to bed," I responded.

"Okay, just ignore him, you know he has no sense," Anthony replied.

Finally, all done. I squeezed out the remainder of water in the dish cloth, folded the cloth in two, and placed it under the kitchen cupboard on top of the drain.

I turned off the kitchen light and headed upstairs to my bed.

I opened my bedroom door and closed it softly.

Not even seconds later I heard someone at my door and even before I released my breath, he was in my room standing and staring at me.

He walked over to me, holding his manhood and squeezing it.

He reached towards me and touched my private part, and I didn't even flinch or move this time.

"I need to buss and when Anthony goes into the shower mi ah come back," Ricky said.

I knew what buss meant from a young age, it's the Jamaican way of saying "I need to cum."

I kept staring at him with my eyes dry, with no tears in my eye sockets as if everything in me is dried up, and watched him leave my room without blinking.

I used to hear my mom and Tony say they can tell when a girl has been sexually active because her attitude and walk changes.

"Has my walk and attitude not changed?" I whispered to myself, "Why doesn't my mom notice the changes in me ever since he moved in with us?"

My appetite is not the same, and I don't even smile and speak the same anymore. I feel as if my mom knows and she's purposely avoiding it. How does she not see the decline and depression?

> "Don't get too caught up in your own world of things that you don't realize the changes happening around and within your children. Pay attention to the signs and be aware of their changes."
>
> —Jenelle Simpson

I stop staring into Lalaland and walk over to my bed. I climbed into bed and wiggled under my sheets with my head covered with the sheets. I'm still extremely scared of the dark, so the sheet over my head is a routine thing for me, but I certainly feel less fearful and know now that the dark is harmless.

I think to myself, what's the point of going to sleep when he's going to creep in here and wake me up?

Mom always comes into our rooms to check on us, give us a rub on our foreheads, and say a quick little prayer over us for God's protection.

What I don't understand is why she always comes before or after he has already mutilated me.

Aren't moms supposed to have an extra "children sense" where they can feel or pick up on something when things aren't right with their children?

I guess my mom didn't get that extra sense.

I clenched my body tightly under my sheets and started thinking about when I become a teenager and turn eighteen. When I move out, meet my boyfriend, and start my family.

My boyfriend is going to be tall, with brown skin and an athletic tone. He's going to be bad, sexy, strong, a money maker, smart, and a business owner.

I started smiling from ear-to-ear, fantasizing about when my boyfriend and I move in together in our apartment. I will finally escape from here.

I want someone who will treat me with love, someone gentle, but not too soft, and a protector.

CHAPTER 15

Take Me Back

"I stopped resisting and allowed God to gracefully break me into my transformation and elevation."

— Jenelle Simpson

"*Zzz*" "*Zzz*" "*Zzz*" "*Zzz*" "*Zzz*" "*Zzz*" "*Zzz*" – It's almost like I can literally hear myself snoring in my sleep.

I love dancing and one of my favorite songs is by Garnett Silk, "Oh Me Oh My."

The music is beating sooo loud, I can almost hear it. I feel the bass coming through the big black speaker boxes, the speaker grills are bouncing, and I can feel the sound rushing through my body.

I stand, rocking my body to the rhythm of the music, with my bag juice and Big Foot snack in my hand. Big Foot snacks, like another of my favorites, are like Cheetos that are big and the shape of feet.

Bag juice, my favorite drink! So yummy and refreshing.

I really love going to the shop with my dad and *holding a meds* (vibing). Spending time with my dad means so much to me, because that's our special time and I am my dad's "likkle" general.

Mom would always say, "Yuh just like yuh fada." (You and your father are just alike).

My dad is my twin; I have an old soul just like him and we love the same genre of music.

Anthony is standing beside my uncles, Bobby, Mikey, Riley and Buju. They're trying to chat up some girls.

"Daddy, Daddy!" I yelled out and ran over to my dad.

"Yes mumz," Daddy replied.

"Mi cyaan have another bag juice please?" I replied.

"Yea mon, go ask the bar man fi one more," Dad replied.

"Beg yuh one bag juice please," I ask the bar man.

He handed the bag juice to me, and I take it with an excited look on my face. I run over to my Aunty Kim and her school friends.

I can feel something heavy beside me. I can smell the strong scent of oils and men's body wash.

I jumped up out of my bed and inhaled in shock. It's him, he's in my bed right beside me with his hand over my mouth, securing me from screaming out.

I could hear the shower running; Anthony must be in there taking a shower.

"Mi nuh tell yuh fi wait up fi mi," he said.

He had this aching look in his eyes like he was in pain and needed to be released. I felt like I was looking into hell.

I stare at him speechless as he runs his hands down my pants and forces them off.

Tonight, I plan to put up one hell of a fight, I clench my legs tight together as he tries to separate my legs. He digs his nails into my legs and squeezes them in hopes that I would let go and open up.

He finally stops pulling, grabs his private and forces it between my legs, pulling at the tiny hairs growing on my vagina. He thrusts his body up and down on top of me, trying to wiggle his way in between my legs so he can reach inside of me, but I continue to squeeze my legs tighter and I am not easing up.

"Yuh ah guh mek me dick rip," he whispers in a loud, aggressive but calm voice.

"Open up yuh legs and stop ramp wid me," he said.

He continues to go up and down as I feel his private getting hard, firm and stronger.

I have never seen a man's private, his is my first and it's disgusting. It's long, dark, thick, and veiny.

My legs are starting to feel weaker and weaker as he uses full force and both hands to pull my legs open and there it is, he slides right inside of me and I feel like I just lost myself again.

He puts his face on my neck, and I can feel him breathing heavily on my neck.

"Yuh like it?" he questioned.

I don't respond, but tears are running down my face.

He starts to go harder and harder.

It hurts so bad I want to scream and make some sort of noise, but I actually don't know how. At one point it felt good, bad good.

"Ughhh," I opened my mouth and released a sound I have never released before.

"Yuh like it?" he questioned again.

"No, get off me I hate you, you are nasty," I finally opened my mouth and responded to his psychopathic question.

I can feel something release inside of me.

"Ahhhhh mmmm," he makes some nasty sexual sounds as he cums inside of me.

He gets up off of me and throws a piece of clothing on me, telling me to wipe myself off.

He left the room quickly and didn't say anything. He got what he wanted and rushed out before Anthony could catch him leaving my room.

I lay in my bed crying and feeling so much hate for my mom.

I need her to protect me and hear me without me saying words. Why doesn't Mommy see me, I questioned God and myself.

I close my eyes with tears flowing like Niagara Falls, trying to put myself to sleep.

"Children have silent cries; you have to be in tune and feel those silent words through their eyes. Connect with your children spiritually and understand when something is happening without them screaming out to you. Build a relationship, not a routine."

— Jenelle Simpson

CHAPTER 16

Saturday

"I used to feel awkward when I received compliments in the presence of certain people, because I noticed their discomfort and I was concerned about their feelings. Accept your compliments with grace and stop rejecting them just because the person next to you can't handle your greatness; let them deal with their own feelings and you love on yourself."

— Jenelle Simpson

COMMITMENT TO A DECEITFUL LIAR

I can hear the music playing downstairs; my mom is playing Beres Hammond, one of my favorite reggae artists. The song is called, "Putting Up Resistance." His music makes me smile, and reminds me of my dad and being in Jamaica.

When we all lived together (my mom, my dad, Anthony and I), my dad would always turn on his BIG sound system that he had brought with him to Canada from Jamaica and play the best tunes and sip on his rum and water. Daddy loved his rum and water; he is so laid back, nothing bothers him and he does no wrong to anyone. He's like a gangster saint.

It's Saturday morning and the music is beating so loud but smooth that it wakes me up, so we know what that means: cleaning day, music blasting, big breakfast, and soup for dinner.

It's a routine; Mom does her deep cleaning on Saturdays, and we have to clean with her or we get cussed out.

Uncle Tony and Mom don't allow us to sleep past 9:00 a.m. and if we try, Uncle Tony will cuss up a storm and stomp his feet around the house like he is Yokozuna (the wrestler from WWE), and for a matter of fact he even looks like Yokozuna.

Uncle Tony says, "the early bird catches the first worm," which means if we wish to acquire the best out of life, we cannot spend our time loitering while others are toiling. Uncle Tony always pressures us, yet he is the laziest person in the house. He doesn't help wash the dishes, doesn't sweep or mop the floors, doesn't even do laundry, and man he never cooks a meal for anyone, yet he sets rules and orders.

Anthony isn't scared of Uncle Tony, but I certainly am, so I make sure I jump out of bed as soon as morning comes.

I got out of my bed, walked over to my dresser, looked in the mirror and straightened myself. I shook myself a few times.

I changed my clothes and headed into the bathroom, washed my face with my African black soap (it is the ash of locally harvested African plants and dried peels which gives the soap a characteristic dark black color), brushed my teeth, and put on my IKB face cream (it's a skin care product that originated in Lagos, Africa; it's a skin-brightening Arbutin complex with nourishing properties of vitamin E, promoting luminous skin) that Mom gave to me. Mom says black soap and the IKB cream will keep my face nice and clean, and my skin tone even and not black and dark.

I think Mom has an issue with dark-skinned people, because she always emphasized how brown, clean, and pretty my skin was and that I should use the IKB cream to brighten my skin tone. To me, brighten means to bleach my skin color to be lighter. For Jamaicans, the colour of their skin plays a big factor in all aspects of life and they practice bleaching their skin. People apply chemicals to their skin to lighten its color and believe that doing this will make them more beautiful and accepted.

Colorism is a major issue throughout the Jamaican community and the majority of Jamaican women are convinced that the lighter their skins are the more socially accepted they will be. Ironically, I've bought into this belief and use on my skin the products mom gives me.

I inhaled deeply before I left the bathroom because I knew I would have to see that "Jancro." Uncle Ricky is the original John Crow and vulture. He's a person that is the lowest form of human and I don't even think he has a heart within him, the way he brutalizes me and watches me cry.

Yes, that's what he is a "dutty Jancro"… nasty!

Grandma Sweetie had the best names to call people, especially when insulting them and sometimes it would be a joke … harmless, such as "Dutty Jancro weh fly pitch pon," a dirty vulture that a bird pooped on.

I opened the door to the bathroom and headed straight downstairs to the kitchen to see Mom.

"Good morning, Mom and Uncle Tony," I said with the fakest smile on my face.

"Mawning gyaly," Uncle Tony responded.

"Morning darling," Mom replied.

Mom had made ackee and saltfish with fried dumplings. OH! And I could smell the milo too, one of my favorite Jamaican chocolate teas. It's like hot chocolate basically, but much tastier.

Mom was dishing out our food and preparing for us to eat breakfast as one "big, happy family." Mom always made sure we ate meals together as a family when possible; she always cooked even when she wanted to break things.

"Take out some plates and some forks for mi please," Mom said.

"Okay," I responded.

I took out five glasses, plates, and forks and lay them out on the table.

Mom started to share out the ackee and saltfish in a big white glass dish so she could allow us to share out our own portion of food, but she tended to always share it out for all of us, so I didn't see the point of giving us an option that she really intends to do herself.

"Weh Anthony and Ricky deh?" Uncle Tony questioned.

"Anthony is in the bathroom," I responded.

Although I knew Anthony was still in bed, I lied because I didn't want him to get in trouble and them to start fighting again.

Anthony and Uncle Tony didn't really get along. It's almost like Uncle Tony was pretending to like Anthony for show for mom, but he spoke to Anthony as if he didn't like him and treated him very poorly.

I remember when we used to live in our apartment in Scarborough, Anthony accidentally ran over my foot with a shopping cart while we were shopping. I still have a scar on the side of my ankle. When we got home, Uncle Tony beat him in the middle of his hand with a plastic hanger. Anthony didn't intentionally hit me with the cart, but I could tell that Uncle Tony wanted a reason to get mad and beat Anthony for some strange reason. It's almost as if he took pleasure out of hurting us.

I can't really remember if that was the first, second, or even third time Uncle Tony put his hands on Anthony, but that was the first time Anthony stood up for himself and that was the day everything changed. Anthony was upset and hurt, and although he cried, he handled it like it was nothing.

The entire family was mad, and my grandma called our dad, but he didn't show up to take us away from there.

The way Dad was mad and ragging on the phone, we were positive that he was coming to get us and we wouldn't have to live there anymore.

Not seeing him show up made me feel like he didn't care about us and that he was a coward. Anthony and I never spoke about that day so I'm not sure how he felt, but I know he was bothered ... unhappy.

My entire family, especially my grandma, can't understand why my mom would allow a man who is not our father to lay hands on us and have so much control of us.

As I've said, we rarely see our dad because Uncle Tony and Mom don't allow us to. It's been months but feels like years, and sometimes literally years go by and we don't see him... Mom makes it seem like Dad is a deadbeat and he doesn't do anything for us, but he does. I know he gives her money, what he can afford, and he has taken Anthony and I shopping for clothes. What Dad does for us isn't enough for Mom, so she just makes him look bad and down talks him.

"The greatest thing is when a person cares and genuinely does the best they can do for their children. Separation is not easy, especially when there is infidelity and pain involved, however don't let your personal emotions spill over onto the children and affect their relationship with either parent. Allow children to grow, create their own relationship with their parent and not force things down their throat. Deal with yourself first, heal, grow past your expired emotions and give your children the gift of choice and truth."

– Jenelle Simpson

CHAPTER 17

Rooted Dysfunction

"I apologized to myself for allowing certain things to happen to me, but I also hugged and thanked myself for being strong, allowing myself to go through the healing stages and to receive change.

Acknowledge yourself and your strength; you deserve to be praised by yourself."

— Jenelle Simpson

It's almost like Uncle Tony is trying to keep us away from our entire family and doesn't want us to have a relationship with them at all. He claims our family is wicked, and apparently they "dislike" him for no reason, but I know otherwise.

Almost every weekend we used to go spend time with my Aunty Korraine and spend the entire weekend at her house. She's my favorite aunt and always there when I need her. Ever since Uncle Tony and Mom started dating, everything shifted — Mom changed. The bond she had with her sisters, or really all of her siblings, doesn't exist anymore, and she seems way too fine with that.

> "Family is so important and no matter what the circumstances are, we have to learn to put our differences aside, build a rock-solid relationship and learn to love each other unconditionally despite our differences. Never allow anyone to drive distance or take away your opportunity to mend, heal, communicate, grow and love on your family. Take the time to dig deep and grow together. We are human and we will never be perfect, but we can change and work on those areas."
>
> - Jenelle Simpson

They all distanced themselves from her, and Aunty Korraine is the only sister who speaks to Mom along with her other sister back in Jamaica, Paulette. Aunty Korraine and Mom speak on the down low. Mom forwards her mail to Aunty Korraine's house, because Mom has important private mail that she doesn't want Uncle Tony to see. Aunty Korraine loves Mom; their relationship isn't as strong anymore, but you know that they love each other and are hurt by everything that's happening.

COMMITMENT TO A DECEITFUL LIAR

Uncle Tony has no respect, he's like living with a narcissist who loves to remind us all that "he is the man of the house" and what he says goes. He loves to flex and stomp his feet around, everywhere he goes, so he has to make his presence known and the whole energy dries up.

Sweetie calls him "mama man" which means a man who is inordinately concerned with women's activities such as gossip or household work. An effeminate, but not necessarily homosexual male.

Sweetie didn't like something about him from the first day she met him, and while she tried very hard to see the good in him and try to get to know him, she said "mi spirit jus nuh tek him" (my spirit doesn't really take to him, something feels off about him).

She couldn't stand the sight of him and whenever he was around her, which is rarely now, she leaves the room and doesn't say a word to him.

Uncle Tony hated when Sweetie didn't greet him; he would cuss at Mom and

let her know that "her mother should respect him, he is the man and she must greet him in his own house and he doesn't want her in his house unless she learns to respect him and apologize.

Sweetie would never after apologize to him for anything ... NEVER, because she meant to disrespect him, and she directly wanted him to know that she has not even a drip of respect for him.

Uncle Tony emphasizes how the house belongs to him, but his name is not on title to the property. Mom's name and his aunt's name is on the mortgage and the property.

He is very vulgar, loud, and bossy. He has no respect for Grandma Sweetie and curses a lot of bad words in front of everyone and anyone with zero care how they feel about it or how it affects them.

When Grandma used to come over to the house to see us, she would pretend that she was sleeping when he came in the house so she wouldn't have to speak to him at all.

Uncle Tony is the type of person to hide around the corner and listen in on your conversations and listen in on Mom's conversations on the phone.

To prevent trouble between Uncle Tony and Anthony, I turned from the breakfast table, walked away, and rushed upstairs in fear to go make sure Anthony was awake before Uncle Tony realized he was not yet. I couldn't care less about Ricky or what happens between him and Uncle Tony, so I won't be saying anything to him about waking up.

I headed upstairs swiftly straight to Anthony's room, knocked on the door, and waited for him to answer.

He was taking too long to respond, so I opened the door and entered without his permission.

"Anthony, breakfast is ready, get up," I said.

I always get paranoid because I don't like when Anthony and Uncle Tony fight, as my mom gets in the middle and I can tell she doesn't know what to do, but she always seems to be on Uncle Tony's side — or at least that's the way it appears.

When Mom and Uncle Tony fight it gets loud; we can hear him screaming at her, telling her to shut up and we can usually hear the hits; although we don't always see the physical altercations, we know it's happening by the sounds and ruffles.

I headed back downstairs in a hurry to play it off as if I just went to get something and so that I didn't cross paths with Ricky.

"Siddung and eat, yuh neva wan eat (sit down and eat, you don't like to eat)," Mom said.

"I do eat," I mumbled underneath my breath.

I pulled out my chair and sat down at the table.

Mom took out a big silver spoon from the drawer, turned on the kitchen pipe, and rinsed the spoon.

Mom believed that although the spoons, dishes, and cups have been washed, they still need to be rinsed off before we use them.

She dipped the spoon into the bowl with the ackee and saltfish, took two scoops of the ackee and saltfish and two fried dumplings and put them on my plate. She passed my cup with milo and a cup with orange juice over to me.

"Mek sure yuh eat everything and nuh bodda waste the food, cuz ah nuff pickney ah Africa and Jamaica well want deh food deh right now," Mom said.

She always reminded us that wasting good food was bad because another child in a different country could benefit from the food.

Both Uncle Ricky and Anthony were walking down the stairs. Uncle Ricky was walking behind Anthony with his big ugly head staring at me. I turned my head away, but I could still feel him stripping me with his eyes.

"Mawning Claudette, mawning Tony, mawning Danielle," Ricky said with a big smile on his face and his gap teeth rubbing against his lips.

I started eating my breakfast, one small bite at a time. Everyone was now sitting at the table eating.

I felt something kick my leg under the table and I ignored it, thinking maybe it was possibly an accident, but then I felt another kick, and I instantly yelled, "Stop kicking me!"

I yelled so loud I didn't realize how loud it really was.

I then went quiet in fear.

"What happened to you?" Uncle Tony questioned.

"Nun nun," Uncle Ricky responded with his head in his plate and nose flaring up with anger.

Uncle Ricky responded fast as if uncle Tony was speaking to him, but really he was questioning me.

"How yuh mean nun?" Uncle Tony questioned.

"What happened?" Mom questioned me.

"Mi foot just touch har suh and she ah mek up noise," Uncle Ricky responded with attitude.

"No, he kicked me more than once under the table," I responded.

"Mi kick yuh, what ah likkle pickney lie, yuh see mi kick yuh?" Uncle Ricky questioned.

"Yuh know weh mi would like fi know, why the two ah yuh always ah fight fight suh, wha's up?" Uncle Tony questioned.

"Nun, nun nuh wrong ah she always ah pick fight wid mi," Uncle Ricky responded.

"She always ah pick fight wid yuh, mi nuh understand weh yuh mean ah yuh likkle niece suh how she always ah pick fight wid yuh?" Uncle Tony questioned.

"She always ah lick me and call me names," Uncle Ricky responded.

"No, he always hits me when you guys aren't here," I responded.

"Mi lick yuh, Anthony yuh eva see mi ah lick yuh sista?" Uncle Ricky responded, raising his voice and going on as if he is the saint in the house.

Anthony stared into his plate in silence, unsure what to do or say.

"Alright done the argument, done done, everybody eat, and stop it," Mom responded.

Uncle Tony still had questions about what was really going on between Uncle Ricky and I, but mom shut him down as if she knew something and didn't want it to come to light.

"I don't know what's going on between the two of you, because you guys are always arguing and fighting, but I am going to get down to the bottom of it," Uncle Tony said in a strong and firm voice.

His voice made me real fearful and I instantly shut up.

Uncle Ricky stared at me from the side of his eye, and mouthed for me to stay quiet, and I definitely knew what that meant.

He continued to eat his food with zero care, but in hopes that the conversation was done and won't be brought up again.

I finished the remainder of my food, cleared out the remainder of food on my plate in the garbage bin, and put it in the kitchen sink.

I went upstairs to my room and started cleaning.

I knew Uncle Tony and Mom had an appointment today; I had heard them talking about leaving to go run errands and go to an appointment, but not sure what it was.

I cleaned my room just the way mom cleans it, so she wouldn't start cussing and going on about us not cleaning and helping her around the house.

I cleaned out the bathroom with bleach and soap, cleaned the sink, bathtub and toilet, and cleaned the mirrors.

I grabbed the vacuum and start vacuuming the entire upstairs leading to the stairs because it's all carpeted upstairs, including the stairs.

I can see mom heading upstairs towards me.

"Danielle, yuh alright?" Mom questioned.

"I'm fine," I responded.

"Mi and Tony ah go out pon the road now to deal with some business, I'm taking Krystal with me so just mek sure yuh behave yuh self and yuh and Ricky stop fight ah yuh uncle yuh muss have manasa to him," Mom said.

"I don't like him, he always bothers me," I responded.

"Alright, just ignore him, yuh know seh him already ina trouble and mi cyaan manage nuh more problem pon mi now. You know seh the family nuh really like me and mi cyaan badda wid dem and dem nonsense," Mom responded.

"Okay," I responded.

Mom already had enough on her plate. She worked like a slave, her family barely spoke to her, and she had a worthless man she takes care of and he treats her like she is his puppet.

I knew now for sure that if I told Mom anything about what Uncle Ricky had been doing to me, she wouldn't believe me so I would never say anything. I just had to find my way out of this on my own.

Anthony had a girlfriend and he usually went there all of the time, before school, after school, and on the weekends, as if they were attached at the hips. As a matter of fact, Anthony had two girlfriends, Olivia and Kanitha. Kanitha is a gorgeous Indian girl, with long dark black hair and a beautiful smile. She and Anthony have been talking for a minute, but he and Olivia fight all the time, on and off, broken up and not broken up.

They all go to the same school, so I'm confused how he has not gotten caught yet for his antics.

I watch my brother all the time, how he speaks to girls and how he finesses them.

He has a way with words to get them to fall for the bait and he's the reason why I'm smart when it comes to boys and I know what to look for now when I start dating.

I finish vacuuming, put the vacuum away and head back to my room to finish cleaning.

I started wiping the mirrors attached to my dresser.

I heard my door open so quietly, but I could hear it. I turned around and his face is as mad as a raging bull.

"Stop act up infront of yuh madda and yuh step fadda, yuh think seh mi fraid ah anyone, mi will lick off yuh face any day and none ah dem cyaan do nun bout dat," Ricky said.

He just basically told me that he is the baddest of the baddest, he fears no one and that he will beat me up and no one can help or save me.

"WOWWWWWW!" I responded.

If he's so bad and brave, why is he afraid of me telling anyone or causing a scene?

I should really just tell, but I don't know what my mom will say, *will she even believe me?* My brother will look at me differently and people will say I'm gross. *How would I say it and who would I tell first?*

I stood there staring at him, thinking of all sorts of criminal things in my head.

He came over to me with his body slithering like a snake. "Just know seh mi ah yuh first and no one can do anything about it," he said to me.

He left the room and I continued cleaning as if nothing just happened.

I heard Mom coming up the stairs; she must be coming up to get ready to leave.

"Claudette hurry, yuh move too fucking slow and mi nuh have time fi wait wait pon yuh," Uncle Tony said to Mom in a shouting voice.

"I'm coming, mi just haffi draw on one pants and that's it," Mom responded in a terrified voice.

Uncle Tony didn't like waiting for mom to do anything, especially when he really didn't want to go anywhere with her. He always creates an argument when they're supposed to go out together and it seems as if he purposely starts a fight with her, so that he doesn't have to drive her anywhere.

Mom is so afraid of Uncle Tony, especially when he raises his voice. I feel like she has no life outside of him. She used to be so full of life, fun and happy, but now it seems like she is stuck in a broken routine. She doesn't even look the same. She used to take good care of herself, go shopping, dress nice, and feel nice, but lately I don't even recognize who she is.

When I'm older I will never allow a man to treat me the way Uncle Tony treats my mom. He doesn't even show her affection or buy her anything. She does all the spending and buying. I've never seen him buy her a gift on special occasions.

He even cheats on her. When I told Mom I saw a woman leaving our house with him when I got home from school one day, he told her we were lying and that there was never a woman at the house. He got upset at me and yelled at me, told me to mind my business and stay out of big people things. Mom believed him, but I was more mad at her for telling on me and allowing him to shrink me down and make me out to be a liar.

Eventually Mom found out that I was telling the truth because someone from his workplace that knew her told her that he was sleeping with a fellow Personal Support Worker from his workplace and that was the same lady I had seen.

Mom doesn't even disrespect his family, but the way he treats our family is ridiculous and he thinks he owns us all. When I first met him, I wasn't too sure what was happening, but I knew that he wasn't my dad. Uncle Tony and Mom just acted as if things were good with a whole man moving into our apartment. He appeared nice, but soon enough his true colors started to show.

It felt like as soon as Mom brought us to Canada, she switched up and did a whole 360 on us all, especially my dad, even though he still loved her, and still loves her.

> "Love doesn't just get up and walk, you make a choice to stop loving someone when they no longer serve you the way you want to be served. Love is communication, patience and understanding, not get up and run."
>
> —Jenelle Simpson

"Danielle, Danielle, Danielle, and Anthony, we ah leave now, call me if you need anything," Mom said, "Bye, see you guys later!"

Now that they're gone and I'm done cleaning, I needed to find something to do so that I didn't have to stay home while they were gone.

As soon as mom and Uncle Tony left, I walked over to Anthony's room to find out what he was going to be doing for the day and in hopes that he would allow me to tag along with him.

"Anthony, what are you doing?" I questioned in a sad and very annoying voice.

"Nothing, what do you want?" Anthony responded.

"Are you going to Olivia's house today?" I questioned.

"No, why?" Anthony responded.

"I want to come with you, please," I responded.

"Okay, let me think about it," Anthony responded

"Okay, fine you can come. I'm leaving soon and you can come, but don't bother us," Anthony said.

"Okay, thank you. I'm going to get ready," I replied.

I went back into my room to change my clothes quickly, so he wouldn't leave me on purpose. Anthony would sneak away and leave sometimes even when he said I could go with him. It seemed that he knew how to play me, to tell me to get ready and then sneak away.

"Anthony, weh yah guh," Ricky questioned.

I can hear his big mouth in the hallway.

He must have overheard Anthony and I talking and now he wants to come. I pray that Anthony doesn't let him come with us, as I can't stand this guy and him tailing behind us everywhere we go.

He wants to be in and around everything that Anthony is doing. Even the girls, he will make stupid comments like: "gimme har nuh" and "mek wi battry har."

He wanted Anthony to round up some girls so they could run a train on them together, which meant when multiple men have sex with a woman one after the other and of course with consent... I mean I hope to God with consent. Not sure why he would want to do that and with his own nephew.

Damn! This man is really sick.

"I'm going to Olivia's house, why?" Anthony responded with a little annoyance in his voice.

Anthony didn't like having him tail along behind him because he's hella annoying, always bothering Anthony's friends asking for a girlfriend and making stupid comments that he appears to find funny, but no one else does.

"Yuh think seh mi ah beg yuh nun pussy?" (do you think I am begging you for anything) Ricky responded to Anthony.

"What are you talking about yuh eediot," Anthony said while kissing his teeth.

"Yah gwan like seh mon haffi come back ah yuh fassy," (you're behaving as if I have to come with you) Ricky replied.

"Whatever, you chat too much," Anthony responded.

"Gwan ah yuh white bitch yawd. Fucking eediot," Ricky responded.

"Suck yuh self pussy," Anthony responded with a voice that you can tell turned him into beast mode.

Anthony has never been afraid of him, even when Ricky raises his voice at him.

Uncle Ricky walked away and went into his room while threatening to hit Anthony in the face.

I could hear the both of them yelling at each other still.

I opened my bedroom door, scared that they were going to fight again and in hopes of calming Anthony down.

As I opened my door, I heard Anthony close his bedroom door.

"Yuh see yuh before yuh stay home wid me, mi just wan lick off yuh face… ah true yuh nuh know who yuh ah ramp wid yuh hear gyal," Ricky said to me in rage.

I stood like a statute just staring at him with nothing really to say.

He was always mad at me and wanted to beat me up for some odd reason. He took all his frustration out on me, and he was always frustrated.

Last time I stayed home alone with him, he choked me and hit me. I didn't want him to touch me. He had told me he would kill me.

He walked away and went back to his room, and I went back to my room and decided to not bother Anthony until he cooled off.

I heard Anthony open his bedroom door and I rushed out of my room to follow him and make sure he didn't leave me behind on purpose.

"Sorry Anthony, you okay?" I questioned him.

"Yeah, I'm good. Let's go," he responded.

I knew he wasn't doing good; I could tell by his facial expression, his eyes, body language, and the tone in his voice.

"We can hide our emotions behind a smile and the things we do, but we can't hide our eyes, body language and appearance. Your true feelings reek and tells a story through your eyes and body language."

— Jenelle Simpson

We went downstairs, put on our shoes, and left. It didn't take us too long to get to Olivia's house, because she lived down the street and around the corner from us.

Olivia was already outside, walking toward us as if she had no patience and couldn't wait to see Anthony. Her sister was outside with her, too. Sometimes her sister and I played together and guess what, today was going to be that day, because I didn't want to go back home until my mom got back home.

Olivia's sister's name is Liz. We go to the same school but we don't speak to each other at school; she's I think one or two years younger than me.

"Hi Oliva!" I yelled and jumped up and hugged her. I really liked her; she's sweet to me, smells nice, and is always so kind to me. Although when she and Anthony fight, she can be really standoffish and mean, but that's understandable. Whenever she and Anthony weren't speaking, she made it seem like I was a nuisance to her, which really annoyed me.

Anthony has a slight bit of a temper with her when she does stupid things, such as "talking to other guys" as friends and "flirting." Olivia is a big flirt and Anthony does not play with her when it comes to her being too friendly with other guys. He has referred to her as a "slut," a person that has many sexual partners.

I don't believe that she does, but who knows.

Anthony flirts with a lot of girls, too, and has a lot of female friends, so I don't understand what the difference is.

Mom would say, "You can't be a lady and do what a man does."

I guess that's where Anthony gets it from, but I believe that you get what you give. If the relationship is so controlling and overbearing, then they should not be together and instead just remain friends.

Anthony and Olivia kiss on the lips to greet each other and Olivia gives him a big bear hug.

Anthony is dressed in his oversized jeans, a big jersey shirt, and his fitted hat. Olivia loves when he dresses like that.

"What's up babe?" Anthony asked.

"Nothing, I'm good! How was your day?" Olivia questioned Anthony.

"It was good, except that punk tried to piss me off. I swear he doesn't know I'll really hurt him," Anthony responded.

"Who your Uncle Ricky or Tony?" Olivia questioned.

"Yeah, Uncle Ricky bout calling me a pussy and white bitch blah blah, him ah eediot and I swear I just wanted to punch him in his lip," Anthony responded.

Uncle Ricky always says things to upset Anthony, always has a smart comment and is talking bad about Anthony's choices of girls whom Anthony talks to. He tends to always bring up Olivia's color as if it's an issue or maybe he likes her and he's playing it off as something else.

"Your skin color does not define your personality, your characteristics, or your heart. We allow people to instill things in us to drive hate and affect our ability to get to know, understand and love each other. Your skin color does not define the person you are or the beauty you have within."

— Jenelle Simpson

"Don't let him bother you, you know he has issues so don't let him get under your skin," Olivia responded.

"Danielle, do you want to play with chalk?" Liz questioned.

"Yeah, sure," I responded.

"Let's play hopscotch," Liz said.

We start drawing the boxes on the ground to play some hot hot hopscotch.

"He even treats Lenette bad, she was telling me he was yelling at her and was roughing her up because she didn't want to have sex with him, so he told her to suck his dick and she said no. He called her a 'fat bitch,' told her to suck herself and something about him being a star and he can get "pussy" from any gyal and she's nothing, he can get better and sexier girls than her," Olivia said to Anthony.

"She called me crying and telling me he hurt her and put his hands on her, and I told her to break up with him, but she really likes him, so I don't know," Olivia said.

"Mmmm, I don't know what to say, man, the two of them are weird and he's going to get himself in trouble. I don't care," Anthony responded.

Uncle Ricky is also dating Olivia's best friend. She's a beautiful Indian girl, her face is perfect, skin smooth, she is very obese with a big oversized booty but has a heart to match. I am very close with her sister Naema, she is also one of my best friends.

I pretended as if I couldn't hear their conversation, but I heard it all and wow, he is who he is.

I looked for a stone and I found a nice brownish and reddish one. We started playing hopscotch while Anthony and Olivia stood in a corner kissing and squeezing on each other. That's all they really do other than the usual fighting and not speaking to each other for short periods of time.

I know they're having sex because sometimes when they are in the bedroom for a long period of time she comes out and she looks a mess like they do on TV.

CHAPTER 18

Don't Eat From People!

I am Still Healing and I am Okay Not Knowing It All!

"Let's not normalize giving people tampered advice from an unhealed standpoint. Let's not project our current state onto someone else who is trying to navigate through their experiences. Let's just be there, support each other, and admit we are still healing."

– Jenelle Simpson

"Hi Anthony and Danielle, how are you guys?" Olivia's mom said. She came outside, happy with a big smile and her loud bubbly but low squeaky voice.

"Hello, Ms. Farkas, I'm good, thank you," I responded.

"I'm good, I'm good," Anthony responded.

"Do you guys want to stay over for dinner?" Olivia's mom questioned.

Olivia whispered something in Anthony's ear, and I know that was her begging him to stay for dinner, because the way she kissed him behind his ear means she was trying to sweeten him up to get the answer or something that she wants. The oldest girl trick in the book.

"Yes, we will stay, thank you. We can't stay for long cuz my momz ain't home and she'll be upset if we're home late," Anthony responded.

"Good, you will enjoy dinner," Olivia's mom said.

"Okay guys I'm going inside, and dinner will be ready soon, so come on in and get washed up," Olivia's mom said.

We finished our round of hopscotch, cleaned up the chalk, and Anthony and Olivia continued doing what they do best together: kissing, hugging, arguing, and making up.

Time had gone by so quickly and it had started getting dark; we had played so much that we didn't realize it.

"Olivia, guys, dinner is ready," Olivia's mom yelled.

"Yes, we're coming!" Olivia responded.

We all went into the house and headed to the bathroom to wash our hands and get ready for dinner.

In the kitchen there were plates of food already laid out with dishes on the dinner table, forks and cups, very similar to how my mom does it.

The chicken doesn't look the same as when Mom makes it, but it's edible, with some white rice and salad that has strawberries inside... mmmm, my favorite. Mmmmm yum, I love strawberries, but I've never eaten a strawberry salad before.

The chicken is white with not much color; Mom always adds color to her chicken by browning it with Grace Browning Sauce.

We sit down at the table. Anthony and Olivia sit beside each other and Olivia's mom says grace over the food, a very quick grace and definitely not as long as Mom's prayer over dinner.

I picked up a scoop of the rice and put it on my plate with a bit of the chicken and some of the salad with lots of strawberries.

I scooped some rice with my fork and took a quick glimpse at it, but not long enough for anyone to notice me staring at it and question what the hell I was doing.

Mom always told us not to eat from people. She made sure to warn us not to take anything or eat anything from people and instilled fear that if we did eat from people something bad would happen to us. My mom has way too many Jamaican myths and spoke about obeah way too much so that we literally feared eating and taking anything from anyone. She associated voodoo with almost everything. It really has affected us because it made it so hard for us to live freely, trusting people and just being kids. I don't even trust friends fully; I hold back a lot.

We would go to people's houses and even if we were hungry or thirsty and we were offered something, we would lie and say that we were fine, but our stomachs would be grumbling like thunder.

I do find it strange that Mom doesn't want us to eat from anyone, but she is always the first to offer people things to eat and keep. Hmmm, very interesting.

Damn! She might be mad when she finds out that we ate dinner here or maybe Anthony might not even tell her. We already accepted so there's no going backwards now, we can't be rude and not eat the food.

I slowly picked up the strawberry salad dressing and poured some on the salad, then digging my fork into the rice again and scooping up some of the rice, I placed the fork in my mouth slowly and started chewing. I chewed as if I didn't know how to chew or as if I was a baby trying something foreign for the first time.

I kept chewing, paranoid that the food wouldn't taste good. I don't quite taste anything as of yet, like the food has no taste.

Hmmm the rice tastes good, plain and no flavor as if she forgot to add the salt and butter because the rice is a little hard in some parts. I poke the chicken with my fork, pull a piece apart and place it in my mouth and pause for a minute ... definitely not what I was expecting, but it's decent, not that bad at all.

I used to hear people say, especially my mom, that white people can't cook, but no no that's not true they can definitely do a "likkle summin summin."

Now for the salad, oh man! I poked my fork into the salad with excitement and drove it right into my mouth.

"Mmmmm, the salad dressing tastes so good," I said out loud.

I had to remember this name of the dressing and ask Mom to buy a bottle for home.

"Oh, you like the salad, Danielle?" Olivia's mom questioned.

"Yes, it's good," I responded.

So, I guess I can cross that myth off my list that white folks can't cook, because this family can. I guess people say that because of the spices they don't put in their food, but that doesn't seem to be true. Everyone cooks differently and has their different techniques and flavorful ways of making things.

Mom adds more seasoning to her food to give it a flavor and that's just the Jamaican way, but this food is just straight to the point, nothing special or spectacular, but it's all right.

I eat my food in silence while Olivia's parents question Anthony, and he responds to every question like the good boyfriend he is.

I don't think Olivia's dad seems to like Anthony very much and her mom seems to have picked up on that quickly.

"Do you want seconds, Danielle?" Olivia's mom offered.

"No, thank you I'm okay," I responded with my pleasant voice.

Although I ate the food, I still wondered what Mom was going to say when she finds out that we had dinner here. Anxiety felt like it was taking over my entire body.

I drank my glass of water fast and steady, but I didn't finish it. I drank the water halfway because anxiety was overpowering my stomach.

We all finished eating. Anthony, Olivia, Liz, and I got up and started clearing the table.

Anthony and I agreed to wash the dishes because Mom taught us when we go to other people's house we should always help to clean up and never to forget our manners. She said it's a sign of respect and appreciation.

Olivia and Anthony empty the leftover food from the plates into the garbage. Anthony and I begin to wash the dishes and dry them with paper towels and Olivia packs them in the cupboard.

We finished cleaning up, washing the dishes, and packing them out and now it's *finito*.

"Thank you for having us for dinner," Anthony said to Olivia's mom and dad.

"Thank you for dinner, it was yummy," I said.

"Oh, you guys are welcome anytime," Olivia's mom and dad said.

"Okay, we're going to leave now," Anthony said

"Want me to walk with you guys?" Olivia questioned as she closed the front door behind her.

"No babe, it's okay, I'll call you when I get home," Anthony said and kissed her on her lips.

Anthony and Olivia love kissing, but I find it so weird how they just kiss, kiss, kiss, kiss. They're so young and already in what they call love. They spend days together. Olivia has to see him throughout the day or she starts whining.

We speed walk home quickly to make it in time before Mom and Uncle Tony get home. If Uncle Tony catches us, he will start cussing and behaving like a raging bull and his mouth is worse than his beatings.

"You wanna race?" Anthony questioned.

Before I even answered him, I started running.

"You cheater, you think you can run faster than me?" Anthony yelled out.

Before I could turn my head, he flew past me and already had reached the front door.

I enjoyed spending time with my brother; it reminded me of when we were younger and in Jamaica and also in our old apartment. We were happy and just kids being kids. We use to play pushcart which is a popular game children in Jamaica play with homemade carts that are used for street vending, to transport items. We use to sit in the carts and push each other around, up and down hills, it was really fun.

I used to go outside with him and his friends all of the time, even when he didn't want me there. I would tail behind his friends and kick them in their private parts. Not sure why I used to do that, but I did.

As soon as Uncle Tony jumped into our lives, I feel like an earthquake just hit us and we haven't been able to repair from it. This can't be what it really feels like to have a stepfather or wait I mean a step-uncle, since that's what we call him, "Uncle" Tony.

He's miserable, aggressive, controlling, arrogant, crazy, acts as if he is our father and he sure as heck is not … did I say he's aggressive?

I still don't understand why Jamaican parents tell their children to call their parents' partners "uncle" and "aunty," it's weird and gross. I wonder if it's only Jamaicans that do this or maybe other races too. But like I said I guess it's out of respect since we're not going to be calling him dad or father. No man can take my father's place. No matter what happens or what my dad does, he is still my father and Uncle Tony can never match up to him.

We rushed inside the house, took off our shoes, put them in the glass door closet behind the front door, and rushed upstairs.

I went into my room, grabbed some clothes, and headed into the shower quickly before Anthony. I showered fast because I didn't want Uncle Tony to get home and catch me not bathed. He would start cussing and going on if I was not showered and ask why we hadn't showered all day.

I headed down the stairs, excited to go make sure the kitchen was clean and neat and tidy for mom. That's another thing that Uncle Tony hates… not even a fork can be left in the sink, otherwise it's hell and powda house. There will be a great big commotion about who left it there, and it will turn into a fight.

Like I've said, Uncle Tony doesn't help with any of the housework, doesn't wash dishes, doesn't sweep the floor, but best believe if there's one item left in the sink, he will wake up everyone in the entire house to find out who left it in there and they would have to go and wash it. I find it weird for one person to be that ignorant and cruel.

This man acts as if he is our father and he has the right to treat us the way he does, but as I get older, I realize that none of this would be happening if Mom wouldn't allow it.

When I get older and have kids of my own, not even their dad can mistreat them, beat them, or treat them badly. They will be my kids and my job will be to protect them at all costs.

I laugh out loud at myself wondering how I'm so young and already talking about having kids.

Uncle Ricky left some dishes and stuff in the sink and of course he couldn't wash up and clean up after himself; he expects someone to walk around behind him as if we were his personal slaves.

I finished washing up the dishes quickly, wiped off the counters, and swept the floors. As I turned around to put the broom back in the corner beside the fridge, I saw he was standing by me with his eyes red and his face looking hurt.

"Weh yuh did deh," Uncle Ricky questioned.

I didn't answer him, but I stared at him with anger and disgust, especially after what Olivia told Anthony today about what he did to Lenette.

"Yuh nuh hear me ah talk to yuh? Yuh see when yuh parents gone, stop run back ah Anthony, yuh hear mi?" he said with an entitled and demanding voice.

"And when mi come in there tonight make sure yuh open up and nuh lock up nuh legs pon me, because mi dick ah hurt me and the other night yuh mek mi rip," he said.

I stepped past him standing like a dirty puppy dog and rushed upstairs to go to my room.

He spoke to me as if he owned me, as if I belonged to him and I had to ask him personally to do anything.

He told me I am not allowed to have a boyfriend other than him, what does that even mean? I'm only a child and how can my uncle be my boyfriend?

I'm not sure what I'm feeling these days, but I know it's not normal.

I speed walked up the stairs, but first I stopped at Anthony's door to check if he was awake and see what he was doing.

"What's up, what do you want?" Anthony questioned.

I opened the door and walked in, but not all the way in, and just enough so I could see what he's doing.

He was on the phone with Olivia, you could tell by the way he was speaking softly and looking like he's making love.

"Nothing, just checking to see what you're doing," I replied, sounding somewhat happy so he wouldn't question what was wrong with me.

How could I tell my brother, my first best friend, what was wrong with me? How would I explain it? Would he say I'm lying, would he think I'm nasty, would he kill him or what if he tells me oh, it's nothing? I kept speaking to myself in my head, it's a thing that I do all the time, communicate and reason with my inner self.

"Okay, get out I'm talking on the phone," Anthony said, laughing just like my dad would.

"Okay, goodnight, hurry up and get off the phone before Uncle Tony gets home," I replied.

I closed the door behind me gently and walked over to my bedroom.

I have to come up with a plan tonight so he won't get to me, but what? I'm too old to sleep with Mom, plus Tony won't let me, and my brother, *sigh*, I know he'll end up throwing me out of there.

I climbed into bed and laid down staring at the walls just wondering what life would be like if my dad were here and Mom didn't do what she did.

> "Our story and our journey were already written in stone, nothing we go through in life is an accident or by chance, but God has a purpose for every step, a plan for every test and a reason for every season. It may look like a mess, but trust God's guidance."
>
> – Jenelle Simpson

When I listened to old school reggae music, it reminded me of my dad, the way he would drink his rum and just play his music and rock away. Nothing bothers that man; he is such a humble, pure, and crazy soul. He laughs at everything, I mean everything and in every situation he laughs everything off, he even laughs when he's mad and then he starts cussing all while laughing.

Dad would say, "Gyaly nuh worry yuh self, God is in control. Believe kill and believe cure," which means, don't worry about anything because God is in control. If you believe in death, you must believe there is a cure.

My dad may not have been the brightest, but he was certainly the wisest and most loving man I've met.

My dad is short, probably about four feet and nine inches (trust me he is proud of his height), an athletic build, dark cocoa skin and clean, not a blemish and doesn't seem to have aged.

I get my height from my dad and my body size, and yet I pray that I get much taller one day, and I don't stay short forever and I marry a tall man, minimum six feet, beautiful and strong with caramel skin.

"Zzzzzz zzzzz zzzzz zzzz," snoring sounds.

I felt a soft touch on my head, some whispers followed by a gentle kiss.

Mom was home and I knew it was her, because only she comes in my room and prays over me at night and her smell is one of a kind. It's like a hospital smell mixed with a sweet fruity smell.

I shut my eyes tight and feel a bit better that Mom is home now and I'm no longer alone.

I can hear Mom and Uncle Tony from their bedroom arguing about something and I hear the firm tone and bass in Tony's voice. Their fighting never seems to end, but just pauses for a short period of time.

I just noticed something — he didn't come in my room, and I busted out smiling because just maybe he's done now or maybe he's gone for good. Whichever one it is, I feel good. For once I didn't feel tormented and angry to wake up. I am so excited to wake up and not be miserable, I feel like a big load just raised off my back.

CHAPTER 19

Sunday

"Stop waiting for karma to show up for them. God has a way of dealing with people privately and you may not get to see it, but it will be done."

— Jenelle Simpson

COMMITMENT TO A DECEITFUL LIAR

I jumped out of my bed excited because it's Sunday and that means we get to go to Sunday school at church. I really enjoyed Sunday school, learning about God, and getting treats.

I felt so happy at church; people know my name and talk to me, they actually listen to me, and it makes me feel like I have a family there. I grew up in church; Grandma Sweetie always brought me to church with her, and we would sing gospel music as I would shake my tambourine. Mom would pack barrels with clothes for Anthony and me and send them to Jamaica when we were living there, and inside were a lot of pretty dresses which I enjoyed wearing to church. My favorite part was wearing my beautiful church hats.

Now, Mom doesn't really come to church with us, but always makes sure Anthony and I go; either Uncle Tony takes us, we get picked up by a church member, or we take the church bus. Our church is a Pentecostal church, so we get to boogie down, stomping, clapping, singing, and dancing.......fun, fun, fun. Aunty Korraine and our cousins all went to the same church, so we would get to see our cousins and spend time together on Sundays.

I opened my door with grace, went to the bathroom to get ready and prettied up for my Sunday morning.

I'm all freshened up and ready to go.

Mom has her old-time reggae gospel music playing downstairs with the boodoom doom riddim. Love hearing some good old reggae gospel music, including this one called, "By His Deeds" which is by the artist VC. Next, I hear another familiar song start, "God Is Standing By" by George Nooks.

Uncle Tony loved the song "By His Deeds," he agreed with the song and believed that all church folks were hypocrites and he would play the song on repeat, but it's awkward that he has such a big opinion on church folks, yet he's not a church folk, but extremely hypocritical.

"Hmmmmmmm, interesting," I mumbled to myself.

Mom has her routine every Sunday and this is part of it, blasting her reggae gospel and feeling good, great.

I finished up in the bathroom, left and walked into my room feeling like I just got released from a dark hole and started looking in my closet for what to wear. Usually Mom picks out my church clothes, but today I want to do it and hopefully she will approve.

I found a little flower dress Mom had bought for me from Sheridan Mall last year. I actually liked it, so I placed it on my bed. I LOVEEEE getting dressed up for church. Mom was very picky about the way we looked and we had to wear the finest and the best.

Mom doesn't buy cheap things for us, she spends a lot of money to make sure we have quality things; even when she didn't have all the money in the world, she made it seem like she was a wealthy woman. I turned around towards my door about to head downstairs and I couldn't believe he was approaching me … hmmmm, maybe he's coming to apologize and tell me he's going to leave me alone.

"Good morning, Ricky," I said with the fakest smile on my face.

"Yo! I waited up for you last night and yuh mek me drop ah sleep, gimme some now," Ricky replied.

He reached his hands towards me to grab me, and I jumped back and yelled: "NO!"

"Gwan ramp wid me yuh hear, see if yuh mek yuh madda and step fadda hear yuh, yuh nah guh like it," he replied with a mean ass screw face.

My heart started to race fast in fear that he would hit me. I remembered when he put his hand around my neck and choked me and I didn't know what to do, but just release my body and let him take control.

He grabbed me, slid his hands down my pants, stuck his middle finger on the lips of my private spot and twirled it in a circular motion.

"Don't move," he said.

"Stop it, I don't like it stop," I said.

He pushed me back all the way into my room and into my closet and forced me on the closet floor, forced my pants down with a fight, pulled out his piece and shoved it in between my legs. My legs were crisscrossed so tightly he couldn't get in, so he thrust his body up and down, making groaning sounds.

I could feel him releasing all between my legs as he stared me dead in my eyes with the most satisfied look I've ever seen.

"You know you like it, next time nuh lock up yuh legs pon mi or else mi ah guh punch punch yuh up," he said.

He got up, pulled up his pants quickly and I just lay there staring at him and wishing death upon him. Maybe get hit by a car or die in his sleep.

"Get up before yuh madda, Tony or Anthony catch yuh," he said with a scared voice and afraid that he would finally get caught, but I did not move.

He reached down and pulled me up off the floor, and I let him pull my body up and carry all my dead weight as he tried to pull my pants up for me.

I snapped out of my daze as he walked away, and I walked to the bathroom. I closed the bathroom door and sat on the toilet seat for a bit thinking, but I didn't know what exactly I was thinking about. It's almost as if my mind was in an empty state and I didn't even know where I was or if I was dreaming.

I needed to be woken up because I couldn't believe I was such a foolish child.

Again I remembered how my aunties taught me that if anyone touched me down there, I should tell them and not be afraid, so why am I so afraid? Because it's their brother, or because they may not believe me, or am I saving my family from this disgrace and shame? I knew when my aunts told me this it was because of Uncle Tony. They think he's a pedophile and want to make sure that I tell them if something is going on because they hate him that much. He has never touched me or looked at me in any suspicious way.

It's almost like they want to hear that he did something bad to me so they can crucify him for it and then gloat in Mom's face, but too bad for them it's not him.

I felt so disgusted and ashamed of myself. Why was I afraid of the creep?

I wet my bath rag and soaped it up, took it and wiped down the area where he released himself. I rinsed out the rag, folded it back and placed it on the bathtub ledge.

I shook myself and left the bathroom with a smile as if nothing had happened and headed downstairs to see Mom.

"Good morning Mom, Uncle Tony," I said, "Mom, are we going to church today?"

"No, but that's alright the good Lord will bless me with my license and a car one day suh mi nuh haffi depend pon nuh body," Mom replied.

"Shut the fuck up, if yuh know wah good fi yuh," Tony said to Mom. "All yuh do ah chat chat chat and run off your mouth until summin happen to yuh, gwan fuck yuh self."

Mom continued to mumble under her breath and talk about how God will provide for her and she doesn't want anyone to mistreat her, because she works hard for her money.

"My money buy dat car and yuh wan come disrespect me! Ah nuh suh tings guh, no sankey nah sing so but mi know weh mi ah guh do."

"Shut yuh fucking mouth yuh deaf or wah. Yuh cyaan do nun," Tony screamed at Mom and made sure she understood.

Looks like we won't be going to church today.

Mom doesn't have a license, so unfortunately she doesn't have a car of her own and she relies solely on Tony to drive her everywhere she needs to go. Otherwise, she takes the bus, taxis, or begs a ride from someone.

When I turn sixteen years old, that's the first thing I'm going to do — get my license and next get my own car. It must be hard relying on someone to drop you and pick you up everywhere you go. It's almost like Tony likes owning my mom's freedom and whereabouts.

I don't even see Mom hang out with her friends like she did before she hooked up with Uncle Tony.

He has a say in everything she does; she tells him every and anything, but she hides things, too. She has money she hides away from him sometimes which doesn't make sense, because I believe when you love someone and you have a partnership with them, why would you have secrets and things you hide from each other?

I know I'm way too young to be worrying about and talking about this stuff, but I feel like I'm an old soul, you know reincarnated or something. I like family unions, I love *love*, and I dream about what I want my family to look like when I grow up — and it won't be anything like this.

This family is the perfect example of what I don't want to be like when I grow up.

Tony is the mirror image of what I will never allow to enter my life when I become Mom's age. I look at her as both strong, naïve, and stupid and hopeless. She should have stayed with my dad. I've never heard her argue or fight with my dad before except when she cheated on Dad with Tony and lied that Dad had hit her and Tony wanted to flex his "big" muscles and he threw my dad out. I heard loud noises coming from down the other half of the hallway of our old apartment, but never saw what happened except blood in the staircase.

Sometimes I really believe that Tony is my mom's karma for the way she treated my dad and threw him out on the streets.

> "For every action there are consequences; your actions decide the reaction you will receive. Whatever energy you exhale you will inhale."
>
> – Jenelle Simpson

This is what they do, argue, curse each other out and then we see them talking and laughing up a storm, but we never know or understand what is happening.

I remember when we were living in Scarborough, Anthony and I were at camp and the camp teacher told us that we were going to be picked up by our aunty, because Mom and Uncle Tony were at the hospital and an incident had happened.

Mom and Uncle Tony had been fighting and Mom had taken the oversized glass dalmatian dog statue that we'd had in our bathroom and had thrown it at him. The glass statue hit the inside of his left forearm and sliced it open. He had to get over twenty stitches on his arm. Mom and Uncle Tony made a joke out of it and claimed that they were only play fighting, but people don't play fight and send each other to the hospital.

It was scary for me, and Anthony made sure I was okay that day.

Tony always sends threats to every and anyone, even my "likkle" granny.

I feel like I am stuck in the worst family and it's a nightmare.

Mom had made breakfast, Sunday feast as always.

"Go upstairs and tell your brother and Ricky to come downstairs and eat," Mom said.

"Okay," I replied.

I headed upstairs and went to Anthony's room, and Uncle Ricky was already in there sitting on the edge of Anthony's bed.

He looked up at me and I turned my head away.

"Mom said to come downstairs for breakfast," I said.

"Her and Tony are fighting and he's going on about how she should shut up," I said.

"Big fat chi chi boy, gwan like seh him bod and him nuh bod. Him nuh want we hold him and beat him in here," Uncle Ricky said to Anthony.

"Mmmmm," Anthony replied.

Anthony is very passionate about Mom, and he gets very upset at anyone who speaks bad about her or does anything bad to her, despite their differences. He's had to intervene and remind Uncle Tony to keep his hands to himself.

We headed downstairs to the kitchen to eat, and Uncle Tony was already sitting at the table eating, dipping his dumplings in the liver gravy and stuffing his fat face.

We all sit around the table and start eating in silence as Mom hums to her gospel music.

When Mom is upset or sad, she plays her music and hums and hums. You could tell that she was mad, sad, and re-thinking in her head — how did she end up here with this man?

We finished eating quickly and put the dishes in the sink as Mom said, and we all disbursed in our own directions.

I went outside to play for a bit with a few friends in the neighborhood and Anthony and Uncle Ricky went off down the street to hang out with some girls and Anthony's friends. Uncle Ricky doesn't have any friends here in our area yet, so he just tags along with Anthony everywhere he goes.

Funny how he has no male friends, but he always has a different girl.

One day I came home from school and heard him in the basement with a girl making noise, and I mean sexual noises. It was so disgusting and degrading the way he just dumped her right after and called her names.

Today went by so fast — it's already nighttime.

CHAPTER 20

Karma!

"When I started digging deep, rooting things out and healing, I started telling my story in a different light. I was able to tell my story from a place of happiness, wholeness, and healing. Start rooting and deep healing, so your story echoes a shift in other people's lives."

— Jenelle Simpson

COMMITMENT TO A DECEITFUL LIAR

All of us were sitting in the living room watching a movie. I guess Mom and Uncle Tony made up already and everything was good for now.

I could never understand how two people could fight so much, police show up at the door with so much turmoil having happened, but everything is fine and things go back to normal as if nothing had happened. They would just wake up in a good mood like they weren't just at each other's heads the day before and we would be left in the dark wondering what the hell just happened.

Literally, sometimes police would be all around our house, the embarrassment in the neighborhood and Uncle Tony would have to leave the house, but then he'd reappear he's the next day as if he was above the law and there was no restraining order or peace bond.

It's almost as if they just had makeup sex and sex was the healer for them, sex was the apology, sex was the conversation, the tone and the "we good now."

This is something I swear to never put my kids through, something I never will allow to enter my life or my children's lives and I will always put their feelings first. If I ever have an argument or an altercation similar to any of mom and Tony's… God forbid it, I will include my children, make them feel safe, and create a safe space for them to feel and understand what is happening around and inside of them.

I don't feel safe in this house or on the inside; I feel invaded and like something is beating up my insides.

Uncle Tony and mom would fight and then be the best of friends right after with no explanation or apology for what they put us through, but I guess selfish people know no better and only care about their feelings.

Sometimes we all gather together and appear to be a big "happy" family and watch a show or movie and we get along and tonight's that type of night. We're watching some boring movie and I don't even know the name of it.

"Tony, yuh nah go park the car in the garage, it's getting late," Mom questioned.

"Claudette mi will park the car when mi ready, mi nuh know weh yuh ah hot up yuh head fah," Uncle Tony responded.

"The time ah get dark," Mom responded.

"Ricky, yuh cyaan drive bredjin?" Uncle Tony questioned.

"How yuh mean, mi ah drive from mi ah likkle youth and mi eye deh ah mi knee ah Jamaica," Uncle Ricky responded.

"Him nuh have nuh license," Mom replied.

"Shut up yuh mouth, ah nuh license drive car and him ah nuh eediot," Uncle Tony responded.

"Gwan guh move the car ina the garage fi mi," Uncle Tony said.

"Alright then, mek wi see if him can move the car for real," Mom replied.

Uncle Ricky, Uncle Tony, and Mom went back and forth disputing whether Uncle Ricky could actually drive a car and if Uncle Tony should really trust and allow him to go and move the car for him. Mom didn't seem too confident as she seemed to know the capabilities of her brother, but Uncle Tony was certain that he could trust him. Funny how Mom doesn't trust Uncle Ricky to move the car, but yet trusts everything bad he says about me and all the lies. Maybe she knew he was lying and just took his side again to play the good and supportive sister and all at the expense of my happiness and safety.

"Hmmm hmm, trouble nuh set like rain," Mom said with a smile on her face and her big white teeth showing. Mom would always say problems can arrive when we least expect them to. It's like Mom had a superpower and knew when something bad was going to happen.

Some people called her "goat mouth" and said that she caused bad luck to befall on someone or something by predicting or expressing the outcome and trust me, Mom was always predicting the outcome of things.

She has an obeah woman tendency where she was always predicting and seeing into the future.

"Shut yuh mouth Claudette, yuh chat too much sometimes! Him seh him cyaan drive suh weh yuh ah chat chat chat fah, him ah big mon and it nuh hard," Uncle Tony responded to Mom.

He tends to have a unique tendency of telling her to shut up as if she is his child. He talks down at her, not to her.

He was telling her that Ricky is a grown man and should be able to operate a vehicle because it's not hard, but mom had a fear in her stomach that it just wasn't a good idea and Uncle Tony wasn't listening to her, not even for a second.

I've noticed as I got older that Jamaican and West Indian men and women (sometimes), speak to their partners with control and authority, but they seem okay with the dynamic. I truly don't think it's normal or appropriate for people to speak to each other with so much aggression.

Sometimes Mom and Uncle Tony would make some weird remarks to each other and laugh it off as if it was a normal thing that people do.

They spoke to each other as if they were roommates instead of a couple. Mom would make jokes about Tony being sexual with her friends and I just think that is awkward. Or, they would speak to each other in such a degrading manner.

Uncle Tony explained in detail to Uncle Ricky how to move the car, the gear stick and what to do, and made sure he reminded him to brake and slowly move his foot off of the brake pedal and put it on the gas pedal lightly.

"Yeah, mi know weh me ah do mon, weh di key deh," Uncle Ricky responded as he took the keys from Uncle Tony's hand.

"Want me to come with you?" Anthony questioned.

"No mon, mi good," Uncle Tony responded.

Uncle Ricky headed outside to go to the car with excitement to drive, almost as if he was a teenager learning to drive for the first time and couldn't wait to get behind the wheel. We all headed over to the big living room window that has a small sitting ledge and I sat on it. We all watched as if we are watching a movie and waiting for the suspense to hit us.

He's moving the car slowly at first, now at a rapid pace, and the right side of the back bumper is reversing into the bushes on our driveway and in between our and the neighbor's yards.

He begins to drive the car again in reverse and it doesn't appear that he realizes that he is still reversing into the bushes. I'm not sure why he is driving in reverse since he's supposed to be parking the car in the garage.

Oh, wait! Uncle Tony did tell him to reverse the car into the garage, I almost forgot that part. Oh boy, this doesn't seem to be going too well for him, but yet he claims to be able to drive ... *such a big jackass corn.*

"See I tell you, him cyaan drive," Mom said with laughter all over her face.

The car is in reverse, and we don't see it stopping.

"Anthony, run outside and go tell him to stop and put the car in park, him nuh have nuh sense," Uncle Tony said.

Uncle Tony is now making up noise with his mouth and saying, "All him haffi do ah just put the damn car ina reverse and turn it round."

The car continues to roll and roll. By the time Anthony reaches outside and is running towards the car, the car went "BOOM!!!"

It is too late; the car crashes into the left side of the neighbor's fence and it falls all the way behind the bushes, past the rocky hill and hit the ground behind the convenience store which is located behind our house. The sound was so loud everyone had to have heard it and holy crap…it sounded like cars crashing into each other.

I can see Anthony holding his head in distress and then he begins to run down to the bottom where the car dropped.

"BUMBOCLOTTTTTTTT!" Uncle Tony yelled out while pacing back and forth. His eyes look scary as if he wanted to kill someone.

"JESUS CHRIST, SEE MI DID TELL YUH NUH GI HIM THE KEY!" Mom screamed at Uncle Tony.

Uncle Tony was in so much shock his response to Mom took minutes to kick in.

"BUMBO RASSCLAT, WHY THE FUCK HIM SAY HIM CYAAN DRIVE IF HE CAN'T. DON'T FUCK WID MI CLAUDETTE," Uncle Tony yelled out, in shock and anger.

Mom, Uncle Tony, and I rushed outside to go check on the car and Uncle Ricky (I think).

We rushed outside so quickly we forgot about Krystal. Krystal seemed to always be forgotten about, she was there, but our behavior was so carefree as if we didn't remember that she existed at times and she needed extra care. She was born into trauma and surrounded by it; it's so normal.

I don't think any of us took it into consideration how affected she is and would be when she grows up, despite her still being only a toddler. I mean, I still remember things that happened when I was young, not vividly but I remember most and it didn't leave a great impact in my life now…look at me, trying to piece things together. I don't even know much, but I know that I will be a protector and her outlet to talk to when and if she ever needs.

I started to feel bad, wondering if God really made my wish come true and killed Uncle Ricky. *Why would I wish death on anyone's life?* That's not the right thing to do.

"God, please forgive me," I whispered to myself.

Uncle Tony and I ran down the broken side of the fence to see and Mom ran around the corner to get down there. We could see Uncle Ricky standing there in pain, bent over, holding the lower part of his back and crying as if someone really important to him had just died.

I wanted to walk over and ask him if he was okay, but why would I do that after all that he'd done to me? He deserved this; he deserved all that pain that he was weeping about.

It was a good sight for me to see; just to see him cry and feel some sort of pain in his life was satisfying for me.

This wasn't the way I imagined his karma hitting him, and all the while affecting the whole family. This guy was really a curse in our lives, and I guess now they will blame it all on the "obeah" and Uncle Tony planning this to get him into trouble and send him back to jail.

Mom is so distraught she doesn't even know what to do with herself.

"Tony, try move the car before someone call the police. The police will charge him, member him nuh have nuh license and due to his charges, he's not supposed to be operating any heavy machinery. Micase (hurry up) nuh mon, me cyaan deal wid di problem pon mi now," Mom said.

Mom began to cry and I felt so bad. I hated seeing her cry.

"Ah wah kinda crosses dis pon mi now GOD!" Mom kept walking back and forth, talking and crying. It was a painful sight.

I hated seeing my mom cry. I didn't have much respect for her and her life choices, but she was still my mom, my girl, and the woman that always made sure my brother and I were taken care of…health, shelter, and clothes. Mom doesn't seem to know how to care for us in any other way other than making sure we eat, sleep, and have clothing and shelter. It seems Mom didn't get that type of love growing up, so she didn't have it to give to us, but she did her best and I just, I just…wish she took the time out to do research and learn new ways of how to provide and love.

"Yuh fuck yuh self eee, why yuh tell Tony seh yuh cyaan drive when yuh know seh yuh cyaan drive," Mom questioned Ricky with anger and disappointment.

"Mi nuh know how fi reverse, ah him wrong fi tell mi fi reverse the car," Uncle Ricky responded to Mom with a squeaky, crying voice.

Everyone was passing blame onto each other. Uncle Tony looked as if he was waiting for the right moment to attack Uncle Ricky and Mom, physically.

He was walking back and forth, raising his hands in the air and putting them on his head while cussing up a whole bunch of Jamaican bad words.

"YUH PUSSYCLOT, RASSCLAT FAMILY SEND DEH BOY YAH FI MASH UP MI LIFE EEEE EEE," Uncle Tony yelled at the top of his lungs.

Uncle Ricky stood there, not knowing what to say, with his hands on his head, scared of what was going to happen. You could tell he was afraid that he would have to go to jail.

The fretting look on his face almost makes me want to laugh, but at the same time I feel bad for him and I want to give him a hug. Why would I want to give him a hug, anyways? He should have known better, and as they say, "a nuh same day leaf drop it ratten." He's old enough that you would think that he would know the consequences of a mistake may not be felt right away but will eventually have an impact when you least expect it and nothing remains the same.

This is the day that he is going to rot and bear some of the burden of what he has been dishing out.

Uncle Ricky was waiting for his trial date, because he and his girlfriend were caught in her parents' house having sex and her parents are strict Christian parents who had many rules, such as:

1. No boyfriends;

2. No sex before marriage; and

3. No boys in the house…no one in the house while they are out.

He was in the house and that was one of the biggest rules she violated, including no sex before marriage. His girlfriend's parents were at church, but they ended up coming home early. When she heard her parents come back home early and was trying to open the door which she had put the deadbolt on, she was trying to rush him out of the house, but it was too late, and her parents caught him. Not sure how he was caught, but he was.

She told her parents Ricky broke into the house and he was trying to rape her, he tied her up and put her own underwear in her mouth to muzzle her. The police were called by her parents, and he was arrested and released on bail with conditions, hence why he had been living with us. One of those conditions is not to operate a car and he cannot sit in the front seat of a car. If he's caught doing either of these two things, he would be breaching his bail and he could be arrested. This is the story I overheard and was also told by some family members, not sure if the story is 100% accurate, but that's as much as I knew, and he claimed that she was a liar and that is not what happened.

I mean he said that he didn't do it and that she lied because she was afraid of what her parents would do, but I don't know because Uncle Ricky appears to be a pathological liar. I mean why wouldn't she just tell the truth and face her consequences….it would be a lot lighter than the one they both have to face now together.

"Yuh family ah crosses, dem send deh boy yah fi mash up mi life, from day one mi tell yuh deh mi nuh want yuh family ah mi yawd," Uncle Tony said.

Uncle Tony never liked Uncle Ricky, so I was confused why he would let him drive the car; it seemed like it was a set up if you ask me.

I remember when we took a family trip to Niagara Falls just for the day. Uncle Ricky was also not allowed to be near the American border as part of his bail condition, and Niagara Falls is sooo close to the American border, but we still went anyway. On our way back home, Uncle Tony took a wrong turn and ended up right at the American border. I didn't understand how he managed to take the wrong turn because he knows his way around Niagara Falls; he knows it like the back of his hand and we went there all the damn time. The turn he took made us end up right at the United States Customs and Border Protection – Rainbow Bridge Port of Entry. Uncle Tony tried to turn around, but it was too late and the border security officer told us to all get out of the car for questioning, despite mom telling them that we just took a wrong turn. Uncle Ricky was there longer for questioning and they even ended up calling my other two aunts for questioning, because they are also his surety. We thought he was going to go to jail for breaching his bail, but they ended up letting us go after speaking to my aunts. Sweetie and everyone were sure that Uncle Tony was trying to get Uncle Ricky arrested and since that day they were stuck on their belief that Uncle Tony wanted Uncle Ricky to be in jail or dead.

The entire family believed that Uncle Tony had a vendetta against Uncle Ricky.

Before Mom could ask Uncle Tony to move the car again and before we knew it, there was a flood of police surrounding us; not just one, not two, and definitely not three, but approximately six to eight cars rolled up as if they were about to do a drug raid. As the police cars surrounded us, and we could see some of the neighbors standing at the top the hill where the car had fallen from just staring at us and talking.

This had to be one of the most embarrassing days of my life. I thought when Cory made fun of me at school and attached the name "pineapple head" to me that was an embarrassment. But this is just shameful and disgraceful. How do you crash a car into your neighbor's fence? Did he not see that the car was in reverse, or maybe he thought "R" meant something else, but what exactly?

Yet here we were standing frozen and not knowing what to do; Mom looks like death is waiting at her door and standing still like a light post with fret and worry on her face.

I knew she saw the police, but I think her mind was crowded and stuck in worry mode, so she didn't know what to do as she stood there in fear of what was going to happen next to her brother and Uncle Tony.

She walked over to Uncle Tony, trying to calm him down again, and I could hear her telling him to tell the police he was the one driving the car.

"Duh (please) tell them seh ah you did ah drive the car, mi nuh wan nun happen to him and yuh know seh him ina trouble already and mi cyaan tek the headache pon mi Tony," Mom said, with agony in her voice.

Mom pleaded with Uncle Tony. She did everything possible to try to and convince him to tell the police that he was the one driving the car. She tried her best to persuade him to take the blame, everything would be fine and all he has to say was he felt like he was having a heart attack or something and that's what caused the accident.

"Move from beside me, mi nah tell dem dat. Yuh muss pussyclot mod and raise my insurance….mek dem tek him ah jail mi nuh bloodclot care," Uncle Tony responded angrily.

Mom walked over to Anthony and me as she looked like her whole soul had just left her body.

"Go up, go up, call yuh aunty dem and Sweetie," Mom yelled in fear for her brother and man (Uncle Tony).

I rushed up to the house with Anthony to call everyone.

Anthony called Aunty Korraine and Grandma Sweetie. We had to call them a few times before they answered the phone. Sweetie usually goes to bed early and so does Aunty Korraine.

Aunty Korraine said she was coming, and she did not hesitate, but she was scared.

Anthony and I rushed back down to see what was happening.

As we approached the scene, we saw Uncle Tony trying to walk to his car to take out some papers, because we hear him saying he wants to go to his car to get papers, but the police won't let him, and he won't stop attempting to get to the car.

"Calm dung nuh Tony, mek the police do weh dem ah do," Mom said.

"Don't fucking talk to me, mi will mash yuh up too," Uncle Tony responded to Mom.

"Look pon mi car….LOOK PON MI FUCKING CAR," Uncle Tony yelled with rage while pacing back and forth.

Uncle Tony continues to try to get to his car and does not listen to a word the police are saying, and still the police won't let him approach the car.

Tony has an authority problem. He thinks he is above everyone and that included the law. He is very stubborn and persistent, too.

"Tony, it done gone bod already just mek the police tek the car and we can take out the papers later," Mom said.

"Mi hafto get mi important documents outta the car," Uncle Tony said to the policemen.

About five to six of the police officers continued to tell him that he cannot touch the car, to step away from the car and it's now police property. They try to explain that the car will need to be impounded and he can come to the collision center to take out his belongings at a later date.

"Any important documents you need to take out of the car, you will need to come down to the collision center and take them," the policeman said.

"No, no, I need to get the papers out and your car where, annuh you guys buy it ah my car," Uncle Tony responds with rage and attitude.

"Sir, please stop or else we will have to arrest you," the policeman responded again, "This is our final warning otherwise we are going to put on the cuffs on you."

Uncle Tony still continued to force his way to get to the car.

COMMITMENT TO A DECEITFUL LIAR

The car means so much to Uncle Tony because it's new; he hasn't had it for that long and it's been the car he had wanted for so long: a Honda Accord, dark green, four-door sedan.

"NOOOOO, STOP IT STOP IT, DON'T HURT HIM," Mom screamed out with tears rolling down her face, scared about what was going to happen to Uncle Tony.

The officers tried to warn him many times and told him not to approach the car, but Uncle Tony insisted and wouldn't give up on what he had set out to do, and that's to get over to the car.

Approximately six to eight police officers rush him, push him against the brick wall where the car had fallen, and were trying to put the cuffs on his wrists, but Uncle Tony was fighting back and probably not with conscious intentions, but it looked like a real tussle. The police were trying to get him to cooperate and stop moving his body and hands away from them. Uncle Tony continued to talk and what looked like resisting arrest, but not really at all.

"Why are you guys arresting me, I didn't do anything, all I wanted to do was go to my car, please let me go," Uncle Tony was screeching for air with a teary and trembling voice.

Uncle Tony became more verbally aggressive with the police officers and now they began to use severe force.

Mom tried to reason with the police while they had Uncle Tony on the wall, but they tell her to back away unless she wants to get arrested, as well.

Uncle Tony's face is hitting, rubbing and scraping against the brick wall, and it doesn't look like he's enjoying it, so it must really hurt.

My first experience of a police and civilian altercation, it's almost as if I am watching a movie. Why did so many police show up and why didn't they just talk him down instead of the aggressiveness?

"Go back to the house and stay inside, don't open the door. Check on your sister," Mom yelled at Anthony and me.

Anthony, Uncle Ricky, and I all rush back to the house, in fear for Uncle Tony, but also wanting to just get away from there.

We get back to the house and rush inside. Uncle Ricky goes upstairs, straight to his room and starts packing his bags as if he knows this is his final day of freedom and he will have to leave.

In my mind I am happy that he is packing, because I will be away from him for good, but my heart is sad for what is happening. I feel so bad for Mom because it's her family and now look at the mess one person created for all. I just want him gone for good, he caused too much pain and damage.

Out of all the emotions that I am feeling the one that really has me feeling butterflies, but yet anxiety, is the fact that he will be gone, he has to be gone after this and they can't let him stay. *Please God, let him go and I will be yours forever.* I start making promises to God I know I won't be able to keep, but I make them anyways.

Uncle Tony isn't the best, but I also don't want him to get hurt, and how will Mom survive if they break up? She doesn't even have a car. Now what are we going to do? I wonder what the police are doing to him.

Uncle Ricky had come and turned my life and all of our lives upside down. *Why did Mom even let him live here? She should have thought about it first before she agreed.*

The doorbell rang and we all jumped up.

"Who's that, Anthony?" I asked.

Mom had said not to open the door, but we headed downstairs anyways to check who was at the door.

It was Aunty Korraine, and Granny Sweetie, and Mom, who had not brought her house keys, so they had rung the doorbell. Aunty Beverly did not come because she and Mom do not speak at all; they haven't spoken since the incident where Uncle Tony kicked her out of our apartment in Scarborough. Mom and Aunty Beverly used to be really close, almost like best friends; they had shared everything, and Aunty Beverly could come over and stay with us anytime she wanted to.

To be honest, the relationship started deteriorating when everyone found out that Mom had cheated on dad, kicked him out on the streets, and moved Uncle Tony into our home. None of her siblings or family members liked the energy Uncle Tony dished out, as he was aggressive and controlling from the beginning and everyone was disappointed in the choices Mom had made.

COMMITMENT TO A DECEITFUL LIAR

She changed as soon as she met Uncle Tony — her appearance, and her attitude towards her family — just completely changed as if she no longer cared about life.

I remember the final straw and the hard nail that destroyed Aunty Beverly and Mom's relationship as if it happened yesterday. Aunty Beverly had come over to stay and babysit Anthony and me while Mom went to work, and Uncle Tony was also over. She was bathing me and having a girl's conversation about not allowing boys or anyone to touch me on my private spot. She made sure she repeated it a few times that no man at all should touch my body, especially my safety spot and questioned if anyone did. She let me know that no matter what she would be there for me, and we shouldn't be afraid of anyone or to tell her what is going on. Aunty Beverly expressed to me that I could trust her with anything and that she loved me very much. Uncle Tony was standing outside the bathroom listening in as usual and when we came out of the bathroom, he started arguing with Aunty Beverly regarding what we were discussing and questioning why she is talking to me about that.

Long story short, it turned into an argument, with Uncle Tony asking her to leave; they argued back and forth with threats, and Aunty Beverly went into the kitchen for a knife to protect herself, because she was somewhat terrified, but yet so fearless. When Aunty Beverly called Mom and told Mom what had happened, she seemed to have taken Uncle Tony's side over her own blood sister. That really hurt Aunty Beverly that Mom would choose a man over her, and since that day she vowed to never speak to Mom again — she is dead to her.

"You have to have those hard conversations with your children, connect with them and be transparent. It may seem uncomfortable to go through rough seasons and talk about serious things, but it's so necessary and essential. Never leave your children in the dark without understanding."

— Jenelle Simpson

CHAPTER 21

Commitment To A Deceitful Liar

"Just because your parents went through those things doesn't mean you have to repeat them. They lived their lives their way and you have the opportunity to live and create the life you want; no more sob stories-get moving."

— Jenelle Simpson

COMMITMENT TO A DECEITFUL LIAR

They each had a depressing look on their faces and were worried for the worst.

Grandma barely said a word to us; it was like she was numb and tired. Grandma is always running for her kids, and she carried their pain and problems as if it was her own pain. Grandma barely looked at me and in that moment I realized what it would feel like if I tell anyone what Uncle Ricky did. They would hate me, especially Grandma and I couldn't live with that.

Uncle Ricky came down the stairs with angry tears as everyone asked him what happened and Sweetie questioned why he wouldn't behave himself and not disgrace the family.

I don't believe this was all Ricky's fault, but he was the one behind the wheel and it was his words that said he could drive.

Everyone is passing blame and cursing at each other trying to come up with a story to tell the police when they ask who was driving the car.

The doorbell rings again and there are two policemen at the door.

They said they are going to have to arrest Uncle Tony for resisting arrest and take him to the hospital for his injuries.

They took Mom's statements about what happened and of course Mom said it was Uncle Tony that was driving the car.

The police left and Mom explained to her sisters and Granny that Uncle Ricky could no longer stay with us, because Uncle Tony wouldn't allow it. She told them to hurry up and take Uncle Ricky.

I don't know how this turned into a fight between my Mom and her sister, because all I could hear is back and forth arguing about whose fault it was and how Uncle Tony intentionally did this to put their brother back into jail and that he is an evil man.

Mom and her sisters always had their differences, but only when she and Uncle Tony started dating did it all come out. They were not happy with the way she had treated my dad, because my dad was good to her and to her whole family. When they all lived in Jamaica, dad used to work and help raise each and every one of my mom's nine siblings. Things weren't easy for Sweetie being a single mother, but she had made do with what she'd had, and she had gotten help from my dad. Mom is a two-mouth cutlass; one minute she says something, but the next she is doing something completely the opposite that contradicts her words. She would speak good about you to your face, but cut you up behind your back—with her words, of course. Almost as if she thinks what she is doing is right.

She is very materialistic and loves to compare herself to what other people have.

When Mom bought her first house, she acted like it was the biggest accomplishment that no one else could achieve (of course it's a big accomplishment, but she went overboard) or as if she was better than certain people, because they didn't have a house. There's a lot of tension within this family because of materialism, choices, Jamaican myths, brokenness, unhealed situations, and control.

Uncle Tony sits on a high horse, bossing people around and my family hates that. They had arguments about whose house and car it was, because they all knew Mom is the bread winner and apparently he just milks her.

They all told us that if Uncle Tony puts his hands on Anthony or me that we should call the police, but fear made us buck our toe countless times.

"Listen, when you get to that victory level and are finally reaping the things that you sowed, stop throwing shade and down talking the people who are still growing and manifesting. <u>Great</u> you bought your first property, <u>amazing</u> you married your soulmate, <u>buss shots</u>, you bought your dream car, <u>congratulations</u> you overcome that thing, <u>high-five</u> you started your business and its flourishing and it's a big deal to celebrate. But remain humble, don't disrespect or turn your nose up at the people who are still not there yet. Everyone's journey is different, don't exchange kindness for 'materialism.'"

- Jenelle Simpson

COMMITMENT TO A DECEITFUL LIAR

Everyone in our family warned Mom to leave Uncle Tony before it was too late; they told her that she should put her kids first and not let any man come and take what belongs to her children. My mom's favorite aunt, Aunty Darleen, before she died told my mom to please leave Uncle Tony. It was like her final death wish was that Mom would find herself, find peace, and leave Uncle Tony.

Anthony and I, along with a few of our other cousins, were at Aunty Darleen's house on a Saturday spending time. Our family wasn't always terrible; we used to be really close, have family dinners, and spend time at each other's houses, but Mom made the choice to choose Uncle Tony over family, so the united family ended quickly. Aunty Darleen got a call from I think it was the ambulance person, police officer or the actual hospital saying that Mom was in the hospital, because there was a domestic case and Mom was pregnant at the time with Krystal. Aunty Darleen was so scared, she pleaded with Mom to leave Uncle Tony, because it was going to cost her life, but Mom wouldn't listen … she can't take tellings.

Some days when they argued I wondered if he was going to kill her in her sleep and that terrified me. When they would fight, I would be afraid to leave her at home alone with him and go anywhere. When we would get home, we knew that he had put his hands on her because you could see her lips burst or the way she was walking — we knew something wasn't right.

Meanwhile, Uncle Ricky grabbed all his bags and left with Aunty Korraine and Grandma Sweetie.

He didn't even look at me and say bye, but he was sad and looked disappointed that he had to leave. He didn't say bye to me, and I felt dry on the inside, and I didn't know why.

I can't believe that he is gone, this is it. This is what autonomy feels like and now I'm wondering what's next. Is he, really, really gone or is this just for the night? I smirked with happiness because his absence even for the moment makes me feel so good inside. I still feel naked even though he's gone, and my spirit feels so burdened for some strange reason. I have all these weird emotions and thoughts floating in my head.

> "Sometimes the things we pray and wish so hard for come at the most unexpected times in our lives and we don't know what to do when we get them. There is purpose in God's timing, but sometimes confusion and stillness try to take control."
>
> – Jenelle Simpson.

What's going to happen to Uncle Tony, Mom, Krystal, Anthony and me? What will Mom and Uncle Tony do about the car? Will he have to pay for it? I have so many questions maneuvering around in my mind, and I can't grab ahold of just one or one answer. Everything is happening so fast, and this is not the way I expected it to go. I wanted him gone, I wanted him to suffer and go through a bad term of karma, but this is not what I asked for, not for my family to be left in pieces, pain, disaster, and more brokenness.

"God! This is so unfair," I blurted out.

Mom looks over at me with her eyes looking like a lost puppy dog, with fear pouring out of her skin.

"It's okay, don't fret, we will figure it out," Mom said.

Seconds later she begins to break down in tears. Mom's cries were loud like cow bawlings, and I hated it, because it automatically shifted my spirit and caused me to cry. Anthony and I both walked over to her, hugged her and hushed her as she cried.

Mom isn't perfect, but she has gone through a lot in life. She works like a slave, as I said, takes care of her home, gets abused verbally and physically and she takes it, and he doesn't even apologize or buy her an apology gift like the husbands and boyfriends do on TV.

I don't understand why she settles for this type of treatment, and she has to know that she deserves better and greater. I love her so much, but it hurts to see her like this, and I don't see strength.

You could tell Anthony felt numb, because he didn't say a word. Anthony is an overthinker, and he uses music to calm himself and doesn't speak about his emotions.

> "Music plays such an important role in many people's lives; it's an instrument, an outlet, and a way to express feelings, but sometimes venting through words feels better."
>
> – Jenelle Simpson

Where do we go from here? I questioned while I stood beside Mom with my hands on her.

I knew Mom would have to go and pick him up from the hospital or the police station, wherever he was, but she hasn't said anything yet and she doesn't even drive, so how is this going to work? I fear what's ahead for Mom and more so us, Anthony and me.

One problem is gone, but we are now left with a bigger problem and a bigger monster, being Uncle Tony.

I fear when he comes home there's going to be a big fight and I fear for Mom's life.

> "Sometimes when you get that thing and that breakthrough you've been waiting for, you don't know what to do next, but trust God through the process. God is timely and purposeful."
>
> – Jenelle Simpson

"Anthony, come walk back down to the bottom with me and Danielle stay with Krystal, we will be back."

I look at her with panic and my heart pounding, and I think to myself, "Why does she want to go back down there and what if something happens to her, is she insane?" Mom's face looks like she just saw a ghost and she doesn't even know what corner to turn to, run to, or hide in.

I don't think the situation has hit Mom yet; she looks afraid to even make one step and I don't see change coming, but I do see total disaster and more pain.

My grandma always used to say, "If yu cyaan 'ear, yu mus' feel." Grandma always used to remind us that if we don't heed the warnings of others, we must deal with the consequences. We must not be too stubborn to listen when someone is talking to us and trying to teach us something, or we will have to face the consequences on our own whether emotional or physical; therefore we must be very careful!

Seems like Mom really couldn't hear when her loved ones had told her it's not a good idea to let her brother live with us. She was deaf to people, friends and her family, warning her to leave Uncle Tony or else she would regret it.

This seems to be her "If yu cyaan 'ear, yu mus' feel" moment and her karma for "biting the hands that fed her," my dad.

> "You can help people on their journey to change, but you can't force change, you have to be content and make a choice to be a continuous help or to back away."
>
> – Jenelle Simpson

He was gone and I still didn't plan on saying anything. It's almost as if I was committed to him and I didn't want to betray or hurt him anymore than he already was. I felt bad for him, and I didn't understand why I was hanging onto this painful thing, and I wished I could tell my mom and she would hug me like a mother should. I wished Mom could see the pain in my eyes and my lips moving.

Mom was tied between her family, and Uncle Tony; she took both sides and tried to stay committed to both, but that had failed and look where it got us.

I am Living Intentionally With Purpose

"It's normal to say, 'I don't know, and I can't give you advice, because I'm not in the best position to do that and I don't want to give my biased opinion.'"

– Jenelle Simpson

Intentional Thoughts: Of course, 90%, if not all of us, give our opinions and advice based on our own life experiences and sometimes it's not always the best advice, because we are reflecting our own life experiences onto others from an unhealed standpoint. It's natural to want to give advice from where we've been but try this… don't give a piece of advice or any input on things that you have no business doing. Heal first and cleanse whatever it is that you're harboring in your spirit before you give tampered advice to someone who is searching for genuine and authentic advice.

Firm Affirmations:

I will not give advice regarding situations I have not healed from!

I'm okay with admitting that I'm not healed, and I am still processing things!

I will not give advice on things I have no experience with and cause anyone to stray in the wrong direction!

I will learn to be okay saying "I'm sorry, I am not the best person for you to seek advice from at this time!"

I have to deal with myself first before I give advice to anyone!

I am learning to be okay with not saying anything and just listening!

I can be an outlet for someone and not give a biased opinion but stay neutral and support them in the best way I can!

I am still healing and I am okay with saying that out loud!

Intentional Thoughts: We are human and it's natural to go through human emotions and seasons in your life. And it's absolutely healthy to continue to learn from them. What's not normal is being the same, living the same, and going through the same seasons in life. We are different and it's normal to go through human stages, feelings, and growth. Embrace humanity and being authentically human.

Go ahead and live "your" freak'n normal life, with grace, not shame.

Firm Affirmations

Repeat:

It's normal to go through life my way!

It's normal to live life my way.

It's normal to not have a handbook for life.

It's normal to do human things and grow through whatever circumstances that I am faced with!

It's normal to be my authentic self!

It's normal to walk my own journey and not fit in!

I am normal and I normally love myself my way!

I normalize having my own thoughts, emotions, feelings, and stages in life!

I am uniquely made, and my life doesn't have to be similar to yours for me to live my best and authentic life!

Acknowledgement

Thank you to the little and big voices that kept me on my 10 toes and from folding on myself.

I wouldn't have finished my first book without you guys drilling me and God planting you in the center of my life. You have all played a special role in the birthing of this book, as well as my purpose, and I love you all unconditionally.

Shane, my partner and my future husband, boy....has this been a long 13 years and counting of ups, downs, fun, and bliss. You pressed me to dig into my purpose and see how beautiful and powerful I truly I am. You taught me how to be fearless, break away from my insecurities, and embrace my beauty and love all of me. You taught me how to stop hiding behind my hair and embrace the beauty of being bold, imperfect, and truly me. Thank you for your unconditional, trying, learning, and growing love. Thank you for your timeless guidance and support and for loving me even through my silent storms. I love the way you love my craziness, my big heart, and our children. You experienced growth and change with me, you showed me what maturity and stepping out of safe feels like, and I wouldn't rather do it with anyone else but you. Trusting God wholeheartedly with you, our family, and on our net journey…adventure and life.

Lauren, my best friend and my "ahhh, this is what friendship feels like," when I met you I had no idea you would have been such a huge instrument in my life and I thank God for opening me up to walk up to you and say the first "hello." I appreciate and love all that you do. Seneca was an interesting year and the year I was blessed with a "authentic" best friend and sister. THIS WOULDN'T HAVE BEEN POSSIBLE WITHOUT YOU, WITHOUT YOU PUSHING ME AND TELLING ME WHAT DIRECTION TO TAKE. Thank you for helping me on my purpose journey and listening to me ramble on.

Jason, my first best friend and brother, you are my light and my keeper. You keep me safe; you teach me when I am wrong and when I should straighten up. Where would I be without you? God knows why he gave me a brother like you, and I wouldn't trade you, not even for a crepe. Love you deeply and I admire your strength and natural love for others. Thank you for putting up with me and being there endlessly for me and your niece and nephew. Thank you for playing the role of my father and my voice of reason. We are going to make things happen together and for generations to come, this was already written in stone. Love you.

Ada, my GIRLLLLLL. When I met you I was just starting my career, and you were and still always remain there. You have grown on me and became one of my closest and most trusted friends. Through sleepless nights and those long overtimes that we put in, you loved me and loved my children unconditionally, and I never knew anyone could love me and my kids the way you do. You cared for me even when I didn't care for myself. We are from different parents, but it feels like you are my blood sister. Thank you for being on this journey with me and I love you just like pork (you know I only eat pork with you).

Paula, my little sister, you taught me some things about forgiveness and what it looks like to re-love. You're always there near and far even when we don't see eye to eye. I am so proud of you and your purpose. You are so talented and thank you for allowing me to be a contact, voice, and guidance in your life. Love up babes.

Holly, my big sister, my sister-in-law, my soul sista, I love you. You came in my life when I didn't know what family meant anymore and believed in me. You have always been my ear and shoulder and I admire the woman you are becoming. I thank you for always drilling me and signing off on the things I want to do and encouraging me to dig deeper.

Patricia, ahhhhh I am truly blessed to have met you. In the midst of giving up, God literally dropped you off right at my front door. I was on the verge of giving up on this book and God connected us on a deeper level I could not have imagined. I wanted someone who believed in my vision to do my book cover and be apart of my team and he gave me you. You blew me away with my book cover, and you blew me away the way you believed in my and my purpose. You also blow me away as my friend and favorite artist. Thank you for connecting with me and always giving me positive words.

To all the people who rooted for me and continue to root for me, YOU ARE THE BEST AND I APPRECIATE YOU ALL.

I'm proud of me for allowing myself to transform into the person I am supposed to be. "Don't stand in the way of your transformation, allow yourself to embrace your change and grow."

Author Bio

Jenelle Simpson is Jamaican-born and was raised in Toronto, Ontario, Canada. She is a Senior Law Clerk, Paralegal, Motivational Speaker, and co-founder of The Village Children Organization in Toronto.

Throughout her life, she has been known for her powerful voice and positive, supportive, and encouraging spirit. She uses her knowledge and experiences to reach people of all different walks of life. Simpson always had a passion for writing and knew she wanted to be an author and use her books to make permanent noise and change, breaking generational cycles and fearlessly walking in her purpose one book at a time.